WHAT'S WRONG WITH HOMOSEXUALITY?

PHILOSOPHY IN ACTION
Small Books about Big Ideas

Walter Sinnott-Armstrong, series editor

WHAT'S WRONG WITH HOMOSEXUALITY?

John Corvino

OXFORD
UNIVERSITY PRESS

OXFORD
UNIVERSITY PRESS

Oxford University Press is a department of the University of Oxford. It furthers the University's
objective of excellence in research, scholarship, and education by publishing worldwide.

Oxford New York
Auckland Cape Town Dar es Salaam Hong Kong Karachi
Kuala Lumpur Madrid Melbourne Mexico City Nairobi
New Delhi Shanghai Taipei Toronto

With offices in
Argentina Austria Brazil Chile Czech Republic France Greece
Guatemala Hungary Italy Japan Poland Portugal Singapore
South Korea Switzerland Thailand Turkey Ukraine Vietnam

Oxford is a registered trade mark of Oxford University Press in the UK and certain other countries.

Published in the United States of America by
Oxford University Press
198 Madison Avenue, New York, NY 10016

Library of Congress Cataloging-in-Publication Data
Corvino, John, 1969–
   What's wrong with homosexuality? / John Corvino.
        p.   cm. — (Philosophy in action)
   Includes bibliographical references and index.
   ISBN 978-0-19-985631-2 (hardback : alk. paper)   1. Homosexuality—Moral and ethical
aspects.   2. Same-sex marriage—Moral and ethical aspects.   I. Title.
   HQ76.25.C673   2013
   176'.4—dc23

                                                                         2012027319
9780199856312

9 8 7 6 5 4 3 2 1

Printed in the United States of America on acid-free paper

For Mark

CONTENTS

1 | "WE SHOULDN'T EVEN BE HAVING THIS DISCUSSION"

I wake up just a few minutes before the alarm clock is set to ring; not wanting to wake Cranky, who is snoring next to me, I reach over and disarm it. I get out of bed as quietly as possible. *Cranky rolls over and grunts.* I go to the bathroom, pee, and turn on the shower. I step back into the bedroom, slide the dimmer switch down to its lowest setting, press the ON button, and back the dimmer up slightly, tingeing the room with light. *Cranky clamps his eyes shut.* I shower and towel off, return to the bedroom, raise the dimmer some more. *Cranky covers his head with a pillow.* I apply moisturizer, deodorant, maybe some hair stuff; return to the bedroom, raise the dimmer. *Defiant stillness from Cranky.* I grab a razor and touch up the spot I missed while shaving in the shower. I put on a robe, return to the bedroom, turn the lights up full-force, and switch on the radio. *NPR blares; Cranky groans.*

This is our morning routine. By the time I finish breakfast and come back upstairs, Cranky will have begun showering, a process that not only cleanses him but also begins his transformation from Cranky to Mark. If you met Mark, you wouldn't think him cranky; indeed, he's probably one of the most consistently cheerful people you'll ever come across. That's because you don't come across him first thing in the morning.

We continue to get ready. At some point I'll move the pillows to make up the bed, and Mark (who can see me in the bedroom when he's standing at the bathroom mirror) will join me to assist. Our bedroom is typically a mess: Laundry gets washed, even folded, but seldom put away: instead, it piles up on the settee, the ironing board, or the inversion table that Mark purchased to alleviate his back problems but instead functions as an ugly and expensive clothes hanger in the middle of the room. But the bed is made each day. It's a comforting ritual, and (since we rarely eat breakfast together) it gives us a moment to "check in": Meeting tonight? Home for dinner? What are we cooking?

On this particular day I won't be home for dinner. I'm flying to Idaho for a series of debates on same-sex marriage with Glenn Stanton of Focus on the Family. As Mark gives me a quick kiss goodbye, he says, "Say hi to Glenn" with genuine friendliness. This is something I love about Mark (the Mark who is not Cranky): he likes people, and he likes getting along with people. And so he "gets" my relationship with Glenn Stanton.

I'm a philosophy professor, a religious skeptic, and an outspoken gay-rights advocate; Glenn is an evangelical Christian and researcher for one of the premier organizations of the "religious right." Glenn and I have frequently traveled together to debate same-sex marriage (guess which sides). If you saw us having lunch between events, you would think we were friends, and to a point we are: it's a fuzzy point, somewhat in flux, but it exists, and it goes deeper than you might think.

Glenn was the first person to call to congratulate me when it was announced that I had received tenure at the university where I teach. We occasionally send each other jokes by e-mail. We often poke fun at each other—and ourselves, in front of each other. We enjoy each other's company, sometimes even more than we enjoy the company of our allies. And yet each of us believes that the other promotes views that are deeply damaging to society. I would say that Glenn makes claims which are not merely wrong, but harmful; he would say the same about me. Both of us have pointed this out publicly, and forcefully, on a regular basis.

This relationship would be odd enough if we were debating, for instance, global warming or the estate tax. But we are debating something that, for me at least, is deeply, profoundly personal. And to say, as I did a moment ago, that we debate "same-sex marriage" doesn't quite capture that fact. Yes, we are debating social policy, but ultimately we are debating whether my relationship with Mark—the one which begins each day with my raising the dimmer switch gradually to wake him up, but which encompasses so much more—is worthy of a certain kind of recognition. Let's not soft-pedal it: when Glenn opposes same-sex marriage, he is opposing us—me and Mark, and countless others like us. He wouldn't put it that way, of course—another point on which we sharply disagree.

. . .

I'm sitting next to Glenn during the Q&A portion of our debate, and a woman is asking a question. No, she's giving a speech. No, not a speech: a rant. A seemingly interminable rant.

This is one of three debates we're doing in Idaho, and it began when, as we were being introduced, I leaned over to Glenn and whispered, "Are we at Idaho State or the University of Idaho?" (Travel can be disorienting.) He shot back a "Yikes, I can't remember" look. Wanting to make sure I thanked the right people, I walked all the way to the front of the stage during my opening remarks, then surreptitiously glanced back at the lectern. Thank goodness—a school seal! "Glenn and I are very pleased to be here at Boise State University," I announced, prompting a suppressed giggle from my opponent nearby.

Now he was again suppressing a giggle, but for a different reason. The ranting woman was technically on his side. But she was one of those people that you wish weren't on your side, because her rant was clearly not winning her any allies.

"You think you're pretty smart, don't you, Professor Corvino?" she taunted. "Well let me tell you: there's a lot you don't know!!!" She then recited a litany of alleged evils of homosexuality that made even Glenn uncomfortable: We're mentally ill. We recruit children. We have, on average, 6,973 sex partners per year (or something like that—I wasn't really paying attention to the details at this point). "You think you're Mr. Poster Child for the gay movement," she continued, "but you're just promoting a pack of lies."

When something like this happens at a debate—and it seldom does, at least to this extent—the guy on the other side usually comes to the rescue. So for example, when "my people" say things that are false and obnoxious about Glenn, I jump in, correct them, and then try to redirect the discussion to a more civil and productive place. Glenn sometimes does the same for me. So now I glanced at him. He sat staring at his notes. I prodded, "You want to take this one?"

"Nope." (He later explained that he felt—plausibly enough—that the sooner we moved on from this particular audience member, the better.)

How do you explain to someone who thinks you're the devil incarnate, that you're really not? I mean, anything you say is likely to draw the retort, "That's exactly what a Deceiver would say!" In such situations, I have to remind myself that the challenger is not my real audience ("audience" comes from the Latin word for "listeners," and this woman wasn't about listening). The real audience is everyone else in the room.

This book responds to arguments against homosexuality, while also telling the story of my two decades speaking, debating, and writing about this topic. In particular, it addresses the claim that same-sex relationships are *morally wrong*, and it explores why that claim is important—to individuals, to society, and to the ongoing debates over marriage and other policy issues. Some of the arguments I consider are put forth by scholars; others are offered by people like this audience member. I include the latter arguments because they're popular, they have gut-level appeal, and they need to be understood and countered. The angry woman at Boise State—her name was Tammy, I later learned—was there to push for an Idaho "marriage protection" amendment; it passed the following month 63% to 37%, along with similar amendments in seven other states that election. (There are now over 30 such amendments across the United States.)

The book is relevant to the same-sex marriage debate, but it's not just about that debate. Not everyone who thinks that homosexuality is immoral opposes same-sex marriage, and not everyone who opposes same-sex marriage thinks that homosexuality is immoral. On the other hand, most people who oppose same-sex marriage—currently about half of all Americans—do so because of underlying moral objections. Part of what marriage does is give a public "seal of approval" to relationships, and people are naturally reluctant to do that for relationships they view as fundamentally wrong. What's more, there are many people who believe that there's something wrong with homosexuality—something "queer," we might say—even though they wouldn't go so far as to say that it's *morally wrong*. One goal here is to sort through some of these attitudes and judgments.

In this initial chapter, "We Shouldn't Even Be Having This Discussion," I discuss the parameters of the moral debate and make a positive case for the good of same-sex relationships. In the second chapter, "God Said It, I Believe It, That Settles It," I explore religious arguments against homosexuality and discuss their relevance to both morality and public policy. In the third chapter, "A Risky Lifestyle," I make some general points about the harm arguments against homosexuality, and in the fourth chapter, "It's Not Natural," I address the natural law arguments against homosexuality. In the fifth chapter, "Born This Way?" I explore the (ir)relevance of scientific research on sexual orientation to homosexuality's moral status and distinguish the nature/nurture debate from other disputes in the vicinity. In the sixth chapter, "Man on Man, Man on Dog, or Whatever the Case May Be," I respond to the argument that support for homosexuality somehow entails support for polygamy, incest, bestiality, and other taboo practices. In the seventh and final chapter, "Bigots, Perverts, and the Rest of Us," I step back to look at the rhetoric of the culture wars, tying the moral debate discussed in the book to the ongoing public-policy debate over marriage.

Why Argue?

I begin by laying some groundwork. In particular, I want to make the case for how and why the moral status of homosexuality needs to be discussed.

Some people claim that morality is a "private matter" and that, in any case, people's rights shouldn't hinge on others' moral opinions. I think this view is badly mistaken. Morality is about how we treat one another, and thus it is quintessentially a matter for public concern. It's about the ideals we hold up for ourselves and others. It's about the kind of society we want to be: what we will embrace, what we will tolerate, and what we will forbid. And while it's true that a free society grants a good deal of personal latitude here, avoiding legal force except where transgressions infringe upon others' liberty, it doesn't follow that morality is irrelevant to the law. People's moral views strongly influence how they vote, and thus, ultimately, what laws get passed. There's a philosophical connection as well. Laws depend on moral foundations, broadly speaking, for their legitimacy, and the commitment to "liberty and justice for all" is a moral commitment.

So it irks me when my fellow liberals insist that "we ought not judge one another." I understand where they're coming from: Moralistic finger-wagging is tiresome, not to mention counterproductive, and nobody likes a know-it-all. One might also point to Biblical support for the directive, though presumably in that context it means that humans have no business making "Final Judgments," not that we can't make judgments at all. But as a general rule, the claim that we ought not judge one another is misguided—logically, rhetorically, and morally.

It's misguided logically because it's self-refuting. (If we ought not judge one another, then why are you telling me what to do?) It's misguided rhetorically because it makes liberals seem as if they have conceded "moral values" to the other side, leaving them in the untenable position of being "opposed" to moral values. And it's misguided morally, because people have a moral responsibility not only to behave well themselves but also to promote standards of right conduct. The moral tone of society is everyone's responsibility, liberals included.

This is not to say that we ought to become moral busybodies. Humility is a moral virtue, as is kindness, and those who wield morality as a weapon are at least as confused as those who insist that it's a "private matter." But we shouldn't confuse the rejection of bad moralizing with the rejection of moralizing altogether. Morality is too important for that.

Aims, Biases, and Burdens

This book brings together two decades worth of work on moral arguments surrounding same-sex relationships. In 1992, when I was a graduate student at the University of Texas, I delivered a lecture entitled, "What's Morally Wrong With Homosexuality?"[1]—in it, I attempted to respond to some of the most common arguments against same-sex relationships.[2] That event led to a few more invitations to speak, which led to many more, which led to a substantial side career traveling the country speaking on these issues. (My day job is teaching philosophy.) Because I often speak to skeptical audiences, I'm what you might call an *apologist* for the gay community, not in the sense of "Oh, I'm sorry," but in the traditional sense of one who explains something to outsiders.

I write as a gay man who knows something about the subject firsthand. I also write as a philosopher who knows something about how arguments work. As a philosopher, I believe that my own sexual orientation doesn't affect the soundness (or lack thereof) of my arguments. One should judge an argument on whether its premises are true and whether they support the argument's conclusion, not on who's giving the argument. If an argument is sound, it should be sound from anyone's mouth: friend or foe, saint or sinner. But there's more to arguments than their technical soundness. Arguments are tools of persuasion; they are ways of making minds meet. It would be foolish to think that my being openly gay is irrelevant to that. So let me say a bit more.

1. The original title had parentheses around "Morally"—mainly because I wanted to acknowledge that the objection(s) to homosexuality were and are diverse in kind. The lecture is available as a DVD at www.johncorvino.com.

2. The conversational style of much of the book reflects its origin. In keeping with that style, I've tried to keep footnotes to a minimum.

There are two extreme positions here, each of which contains a grain of truth. One side claims, "Only gay people can speak with authority on homosexuality; after all, they know it firsthand." Certainly, any informed discussion of homosexuality must take into account the actual experiences of gay and lesbian people. One common problem with anti-gay activists is that many believe they can know everything one possibly needs to know about gays without ever listening to us. That's not just false; it's bizarre. But of course it doesn't follow that non-gays can't speak with authority on the subject. Some non-gays—including some thoughtful critics of same-sex relationships—study the issue carefully, talk to gay people extensively, and count some among their friends and family. Their perspective on the issue is going to be that of an "outsider," but that doesn't mean that it should be dismissed.

This first extreme reminds me a bit of a local debate in Detroit, where Mark and I live. We reside in the city proper, south of 8 Mile, which has a widespread (and in my view, seriously exaggerated) bad reputation. Some of my fellow city dwellers will try to silence suburban critics by saying, "If they don't live here, they have no right to criticize it." Nonsense. People decide where to live by candidly assessing a place's merits and faults, and unless you're already there, you must do that from the outside. Of course, you can do that in an informed way—listening to those who know the place firsthand—or you can do it in an ignorant way. The same is true for different kinds of relationships (which is one reason this book contains more personal anecdotes than most books by philosophy professors).

But aren't gays overly biased? This is the other extreme: the position that says that gay people can't be trusted to assess their own experience. There's a grain of truth here as well: Everyone's perspective is limited to a degree, and everyone is susceptible to personal prejudice. On the other hand, if having a stake in an issue disqualified people from discussing it, virtually no one could discuss anything. Women couldn't discuss abortion. Nor could men, since they're the ones getting women pregnant. And while I couldn't debate homosexuality, neither could Glenn Stanton: After all, he draws his paycheck from Focus on the Family. The best response to this challenge is to acknowledge that people bring different viewpoints to the table and then do one's best to evaluate arguments on their merits.

(Note: Because I've mentioned Glenn Stanton and Focus on the Family several times, and because some of the other people who appear in this book are associated with major organizations, I want to make clear that this book is primarily a book about *arguments*—not about the moral character of the people who make the arguments, the organizations they work for, or the people who fund those organizations. I mention this because some of these organizations stir up powerful feelings for many readers. Whether those feelings are positive or negative, I ask that you please put them aside as we go through the arguments of this book.)

Then there is a third position, occupied by the large and diverse group who insist that we shouldn't be having this discussion at all. Years ago I attended a panel discussion on same-sex marriage where a conservative Baptist minister made this claim repeatedly. To him, the fact that we were "debating" a topic with such an obvious answer ("marriage is between a man and a woman, period") was a sign of our fallen humanity, evidence of a depressing cultural spiral downward. He longed for a day when "obvious" moral truths wouldn't be up for discussion. He was especially troubled that such a discussion should take place at an institution of learning. And he's not the only one. A few years later, in language surprisingly similar to the minister's, a lesbian audience member made the same point from a different direction: "I'm *offended* to receive an invitation to a *debate* about my rights. My rights shouldn't be subject to a popular vote!!!" (Boise State Tammy is not the only one who tries to amplify her points by shouting them.) "We shouldn't even be having this discussion."

This mentality gets us nowhere, regardless of which side holds it. It's all well and good that you think your position is obvious. But in the real world, the one we actually live in, intelligent, decent people disagree with you. Maybe they're confused. Maybe they're inattentive. Maybe, despite the fact that some of them hold endowed chairs at Oxford and Princeton, they're just not very bright. Whatever the reason, they disagree, and they have influence. They shape policy, they vote, they influence others' votes. Perhaps, in some morally ideal realm, "we shouldn't even be having this discussion," but in the real world, the discussion matters.

I find myself having to explain this point to my allies more than to my opponents. The worst offenders are my fellow academics. "Why do you waste so much time arguing against such a stupid, obviously false view?" they ask. Note that these same academics will complain about the "stupid, obviously false" views of their own scholarly nemeses, the ones they spend entire careers trying to refute in articles and books. Why a "stupid, obviously false" view about Kant or Faulkner is somehow more worthy of attention than one about homosexuality continues to elude me.

Alternatively, smug academics cast their isolationism in a lofty moral tone: "Focus on the Family? The National Organization for Marriage? We shouldn't dignify that garbage with a response." Easy for them to say. They've got tenure, and usually a good bit of material privilege. The rest of the world doesn't have it so easy. Try telling a kid who's just been kicked out of his house for being gay that you won't dignify that garbage with a response. Indeed, this may be the most important reason we should be having this discussion: *these views hurt kids.*

A similar conversation-stopper is the misuse of the notion of "burden of proof." In this debate, one side will typically say that the burden of proof is on those who would limit/criticize/condemn same-sex relationships, and the other side will say that the burden is on those who challenge traditional sexual mores. Glenn, for example, is fond of pointing to the presence of heterosexual marriage "as a human universal."

Both sides are wrong. They're wrong insofar as they talk about *the* burden of proof, as if it fell to one side and one side only. It is better to say that the burden of proof is on whoever wants to prove something. Do you want people to acknowledge your same-sex relationship as a good thing, perhaps even recognizing it as a marriage? Be prepared to persuade them to do so. Alternatively, are you appalled that people present same-sex relationships as an acceptable way of life and want them to stop? You, too, have some persuading to do. Don't care whether you persuade anyone at all, but love to talk anyway? Let me introduce you to Tammy.

Loving the Sinner and Hating the Sin

Some gay-rights opponents claim that they "love the sinner but hate the sin"—a claim about which I have mixed feelings. On the one hand, I appreciate the sentiment that says, "Hey, I don't approve of everything you do, but heck, I don't expect you to approve of everything I do, either. No human being is perfect, but we can (and should) still love one another. And there's more to a person than sexuality." Hard to argue with that.

On the other hand, the "love the sinner/hate the sin" tends to trivialize sexuality's importance. The alleged "sin" in this case is not an isolated misstep, like insulting your sister-in-law's cooking or fudging your tax returns. It is, for many people, life-defining. In my case, "the sin" is my decade-long relationship with Mark, with all the activities it comprises. For better or for worse, I plan my life around it. And so there's a fine line between rejecting it and rejecting me. More generally, the division between *what we do* and *who we are* isn't sharp: some actions and choices deeply affect identity and character.

In a similar way, many critics distinguish between homosexual orientation and homosexual activity and claim that "sin" applies only to the activity. The distinction is both useful and problematic. It's useful because it invites precision: it's one thing to be attracted predominantly to people of the same sex (homosexual orientation), it's another thing to engage in romantic or sexual activity with them (homosexual activity), and sometimes we want to limit our focus to one or the other.

But the distinction is problematic for a number of reasons, mainly because it artificially compartmentalizes gay people's lives. Take Mark and me. What, precisely, is our *homosexual activity*? Sex? Sure—but is that all? What about kissing? What about sharing a bed? What about living together *as a couple*—not just "roommates" or "friends"? What about all of the activities, great and small, that are part and parcel of our life together? What about, above all, our *loving* each other? Gay people's romantic lives, like straight people's romantic lives, include a wide range of feelings and activities. We have crushes—sometimes requited, sometimes not. We go on dates. We call (or not) the next day. We have relationships; we have breakups. We caress, we kiss, we cuddle, we "spoon." And yes, we have sex—though that term, too, comprises a wide range of activities. (There are other ways to wake someone up in the morning than gradually raising the dimmer switch.) Most people who object to homosexuality object to the whole so-called lifestyle—not just the sex.

"Lifestyle" is another ambiguous—indeed, silly—term in this context. Being a jet-setter rather than a homebody is a "lifestyle." Being in a relationship with Mark is . . . well, it's my life. I would never think to speak of my parents' "heterosexual lifestyle" or "heterosexual activity," so why should anyone characterize homosexuality that way?

I'll tell you one reason why people characterize homosexuality that way: it makes our lives sound exotic, foreign, scary. Some years ago, the San Diego Padres invited the local Gay Men's Chorus to sing the national anthem before one of its games. Predictably, gay-rights opponents complained. The Family Research Council sent an action alert that instructed, "Click the link below to contact the San Diego Padres and tell them that baseball is a family game that shouldn't be used as an exhibition of homosexual lifestyles."

Exhibition of homosexual lifestyles? This wording evokes the image of chorus members performing fellatio on one another, rather than singing the "Star Spangled Banner." When the Osmonds or the Judds sing together, is that an "exhibition of heterosexual lifestyles"?

In sum, the language attending the orientation-activity distinction feeds the false notion that homosexuality is mainly about putting body parts into body parts, rather than about life-defining interpersonal relationships. *For this reason, throughout the book I use the term "homosexuality" the same way people use the term "heterosexuality"—as a blanket term that includes a wide range of feelings, dispositions, and activities.* When I need to be more specific to make my meaning clear, I will, but for the most part I will avoid vague, narrow terms like "homosexual activity," "homosexual conduct," and "homosexual practice."

Incidentally, in this book I say very little about transgender, a distinct topic that deserves careful discussion in its own right, although it's often lumped together with homosexuality in the term "LGBT" (lesbian, gay, bisexual, transgender). Gender identity is about the gender (man/woman/other) one identifies as, whereas sexual orientation is about the gender of those one finds sexually attractive. These things vary independently: Transgender people exhibit the full range of sexual orientations, and people of various sexual orientations exhibit the full range of gender identities. Still, the alliance between the gay community and the transgender community makes sense insofar as both (overlapping) groups face rigid social expectations about sex and gender. Compare "If you're born biologically male, you should grow up to be a man" with "If you're born biologically male, you should grow up to love a woman." The similarities between the two inferences are striking and important, even while each group has distinct experiences and interests.

Bisexual people are attracted to both men and women. This does not mean that they are attracted to *everyone* (which would be exhausting), nor does it mean that they're confused, that they haven't decided yet, and so on. Much of what I write in this book about homosexuality will apply, with appropriate modifications, to bisexuality—although keep in mind that bisexual people—like gay men, lesbians, and transgender people of any sexual orientation—face distinctive challenges as well.

The Case for Same-Sex Relationships

When I first started giving my lecture "What's Morally Wrong With Homosexuality?" I heard a common criticism from other gays. "Why is your approach so negative?" they asked. "You always talk about why people think it's *wrong*, rather than talking about why it's right."

It's a fair assessment: most gay apologists spend more time on defense than offense. There are at least two reasons for this. First, acceptance of homosexuality has historically been a minority position. If you want to convince a majority that they're wrong, you need to focus on their concerns. Second, the positive case for homosexuality is, at one level, strikingly simple: *Same-sex relationships make some people happy.* There's more to the story, but that's the basic positive case in a nutshell—the rest, as they say, is details. The countervailing case is more diverse and complex, and answering it takes more time.

Indeed, the positive case is more than just simple: to some people (though clearly not everyone) it seems *obvious.* How do you argue for the obvious? You don't. You point it out and then hope that others "get" it. Philosophers are generally of little help here. Poets, novelists, and filmmakers (not to mention everyday gays and lesbians) do better. Think of the scene in the movie *Philadelphia* where hospital officials tell Antonio Banderas to leave Tom Hanks' bedside because access is restricted to family members. (Banderas plays Hanks' partner.) Banderas's emotional retort—"Are you telling me I am not family?!"—helps people "get it" more palpably than any philosophy tome. The same goes for "I wish I could quit you" from *Brokeback Mountain.*

What philosophers can do is clarify and elaborate. When I say that same-sex relationships "make people happy," I don't simply mean that they're pleasurable. That's true (and important at some level), but there's much more to it. A gay relationship, like a straight relationship, can be a significant avenue of meaning, growth, and fulfillment. It can realize a variety of genuine human goods; it can bear good fruit. This is the sort of thing we celebrate everywhere from great literature to trashy TV shows: finding a special someone, falling in love, building a life together. It's the sort of thing most people want for themselves and their loved ones. In a word, it's the sort of thing we *value.* If you have a "special someone" in your life, imagine your life without that person. *That's* what's at stake for gays and lesbians in this debate.

Conservative critics might argue that I'm equivocating on the term "relationships" here: It's not that same-sex couples share a household or offer emotional support to each other that's the problem: It's that they have sex. These other things are fine, the critics might concede, but they are entirely separable from the relationship's sexual aspect.

I respond that this crucial last contention is false. There is no reason to assume—and indeed, there are good reasons to doubt—that one can remove the sexual aspect of relationships and have all others remain the same. Sex is a powerful and unique way of building, celebrating, and replenishing intimacy. This is one reason why heterosexual couples have sex even if they can't have children, don't want children, or don't want children now. It is a reason why sexless marriages are often cause for concern. To assume that one can subtract sex without affecting the rest of the equation is to take a naïve and reductionist view of sexual relationships. This is not to say that physical intimacy is *always* connected with other forms of intimacy: sex is sometimes impersonal, mechanical, or fleeting. But sex is often more than that, for gays and straights alike.

I do not wish to imply that homosexuality has moral value *only* in the context of long-term relationships—any more than heterosexuality does. For the record, I think there can be some value even in the most fleeting of human connections: the quick exchanged glance across a crowded room; that make-out session with the hottie at the party whom you never see again. These connections are part of what makes life joyful, and there is great moral value in joy. Some philosophers—hedonists—think that pleasure is the source of *all* value. I think they're wrong: there are other important sources. But I would not go to the opposite extreme and deny that pleasure is a source of value at all, or worse yet, that pleasure is by itself an insufficient reason for human action. There are philosophers who have written pages trying to figure out whether it is morally permissible to chew gum just for the pleasant taste of it. Relax, dude. Have a cookie.

To say that homosexual relationships make people happy—even in the expansive sense I've been discussing—is not to settle the matter. Some things that make us happy in the short run are bad for us in the long run (so don't have too many cookies). But the fact that a significant number of people find meaning and fulfillment in same-sex relationships is important. If you think they should stop—if you think such relationships are *morally wrong*—you need a good reason to back that up.

Where Does Morality Come From?

Readers who are accustomed to academics' opening their chapters by defining terms may have noticed that I have yet to define *morality* (or *ethics*—like most philosophers, I use the terms interchangeably[3]). Such readers may be wondering, "Okay, but where does morality *come from*?"

I find the question somewhat funny. Asking "Where does morality come from?" makes it sound as if it were an object, like a houseplant left at your doorstep, rather than an active process. One problem is that the question is ambiguous. It might mean, "Where do moral beliefs come from?" in which case the answer is, "It depends." Sometimes they come from parents, or from neighbors, or from religious education; often they come from the effort to integrate various

---

3. There are ways of distinguishing the two, but none of them is standard or widespread, and for my purposes here the distinction is unnecessary.

sources, retaining what's true and apt and discarding what's not. That's a question for sociologists and psychologists, not philosophers.

Or maybe, more ambitiously, the question means "Where does moral *truth* come from?"—after all, believing something doesn't necessarily make it true. And the simple answer to that question is . . .

Well, there is no simple answer. That's the problem.

Those who think there's a simple answer are usually quite happy to tell you the answer: God. Moral truth comes from God. Okay, but we aren't God. And people who believe in God disagree about all kinds of important things. So even if you think God is the source, you need to figure out what God requires, permits, and forbids. History teaches that that's not such an easy task. Sometimes it's a downright bloody one.

My point is that figuring out how to live is a process that all human beings—religious believers of various stripes, agnostics, and atheists—have to engage. In a sense, morality "comes from" the shared effort to do just that. Trying to define morality in advance of that process is likely to stack the deck in one direction or the other. For example: "Morality is what God says; God says homosexuality is wrong; end of story." Alternatively, "Morality is about people living together happily in society; homosexual relationships make some people happy; end of story." Anyone persuaded? I didn't think so. On to the process.

As it happens, arguments about God are a good place to start.

2 | "GOD SAID IT, I BELIEVE IT, THAT SETTLES IT"

Tammy was waiting for me when the debate ended. I didn't recognize her at first. People's features are hard to discern with blinding stage lights in your eyes, and most people look different ranting than calm. Glenn and I were milling about in the lobby, shaking hands and signing books, when a man and woman approached me. The woman appeared agitated though friendly, and she extended her hand.

"I'm Tammy and this is my husband," she offered, pointing to the quiet fellow next to her. "I don't always express myself well at these things."

I smiled and told her not to worry—all the while racking my brain trying to remember who she was and what she had expressed. It wasn't until she started saying something about "secular humanism" that I placed her: the ranting woman!

Educators sometimes talk about "teaching moments," which here is shorthand for, "Resist the urge to scream, and instead patiently redirect the conversation to a more constructive place." Since Tammy appeared to have calmed down, I hoped for a teaching moment.

"As a secular humanist, you think . . ." she started.

"What makes you think I'm a secular humanist?" I interrupted. I had not announced myself as such, and I don't strongly identify with the label.

"Well, it's obvious," she continued. "If you reject the Bible the way you do..."

"We never talked about the Bible tonight—we talked about civil marriage." (Glenn seldom mentions the Bible in his public case against same-sex marriage, despite the fact that he's a devout believer.)

"Okay, but what's the standard of morality for you?" she pressed.

"I don't like talking about THE standard," I answered, "since it suggests an overly simple picture. But if you want a simple answer, I think moral standards are a function of human well-being..."

"So on your view, *you're* God," she interrupted.

"Not at all."

"But if human beings set the standard..."

"I distinguish here," I explained, sounding too much like the philosophy professor that I am. "I don't think 'human beings set the standard' in the sense that whatever we say is right. Quite the contrary: humans can and do make mistakes..."

"Aha, mistakes!" she exclaimed victoriously.

"Let me finish, please..."

"Okay, but I want to make a note of that: 'mistakes!'" She turned to her husband, who still hadn't said a word. "Remember that: 'mistakes!'" She seemed almost gleeful.

Side note: one of the things I like about debating Glenn is that, despite some of the expected and obvious friction, we usually strive to understand each other. So we don't typically go for "gotcha" moments: the victorious "Aha!" when one person decisively slams the other. This omission disappoints some audience members. "Why didn't you just wipe up the floor with him?"

people ask me, as if public-policy debates should look like World Wrestling Entertainment matches. "Gotcha" moments may be entertaining, but their decisiveness comes at a cost: they seldom convince those who aren't already on your side. When you look like you're more interested in slamming your opponents than understanding them, your opponents' allies will perceive you as abusive, and no one will learn very much. Tammy was clearly gearing up for a gotcha moment. Mistakes! Aha!

"Look," I said, "if I were God, I'd be infallible. But I'm not. Neither are you, by the way."

"Yes, but we have the Truth," she answered. (I'm guessing she meant it with a capital T.)

"Isn't it possible that you might be mistaken?" I asked. "After all, there have been a lot of religious people throughout history who have believed they have 'the Truth,' and they believed different things. They can't all be right."

"Satan is a deceiver," she replied, suddenly becoming quite animated. "But we have the Truth! God gives us the Truth in the Bible!" Her voice was raised, and she punctuated her pronouncements with her index finger. Glenn, who was chatting nearby, glanced over sympathetically.

I don't recall all the other details of our exchange. At some point she brought up something about anal cancer (apparently, a punishment for our wicked ways). Then, back to the general theme: "You secular humanists like to argue around in circles," she continued, "but for us, it's simple: God says it, I believe it, that settles it! You promote lies; we have the Truth!"

"So if you already have the Truth," I shot back impatiently, "why are you bothering talking to me?"

"Right!" she said. And to my surprise, she abruptly walked off, followed by her taciturn husband. So much for my precious teaching moment.

Interpretation

God said it, I believe it, that settles it. It's an appealingly simple picture, not to mention a widely held one. The Bible is the revealed word of God. Not merely a book about God, written by those who believe in God, but *God's word itself.* Arguing with God's word is tantamount to arguing with God—and the "gotcha" moments there aren't pretty (read Dante's *Inferno*).

Before I started debating Glenn (and more recently, Maggie Gallagher, with whom I co-wrote the book *Debating Same-Sex Marriage*), schools would occasionally invite me to debate local ministers. One worry I have about such debates is that they suggest a false contrast to the audience: Here's what John Corvino says, and here's what *God Almighty* says. Guess who wins? (Hint: the omniscient, omnipotent, omnibenevolent one always wins.) Of course, I would frequently point out that we were two human beings debating—each one fallible, each one trying to get at the truth. You can capitalize it if you like—the Truth—but either way, we're all trying to get an accurate picture of the world, and we're all prone to errors. Belief in an infallible God does not make one infallible. Or, as one devout Christian friend put it, we should not confuse complete faith in God with complete faith in our ability to discern God's voice.

I've been referring to "the Bible" as if it's a simple, homogenous entity, but the reality is complex. There are dozens of religious traditions in the world, counting only the major strands, and numerous different (and incompatible) scriptures to go with them. Even within the "Judeo-Christian tradition"—which is actually a melding of multiple traditions—there are debates over which books to include in the canon, which translations are authoritative, and so on. The Judeo-Christian Bible is not just one book, but a collection of books (73 for Catholics; 66 for Protestants), recorded by different authors in different times and places, and assembled—amidst vigorous disputes—during church councils in the fourth century and later.

The debate over homosexuality and the Bible tends to be dominated by three camps. I'll give them names for convenience, although the lines between them are not always neat, the labels aren't uniformly embraced, and the categories are not exhaustive:

1. Traditionalist: The Bible teaches that all homosexual conduct is wrong; therefore homosexual conduct is wrong. This is the position of most Judeo-Christian opponents of homosexuality, like Glenn and Tammy.
2. Revisionist: The Bible doesn't teach that all homosexual conduct is wrong; rather, it teaches that *certain kinds of* homosexual conduct (e.g., exploitative, paganistic, or pederastic) are wrong, and the traditionalist view is based on a misreading or misapplication of the relevant texts. This is the view of many Judeo-Christian gay-rights advocates.
3. Skeptical: The Bible teaches that (some or all) homosexual conduct is wrong, but the Bible makes mistakes, and its views on homosexuality are among them. This is roughly my own view, although I find some of the revisionist arguments persuasive.

This is not the place to explore deep exegetical disputes, something others have done at length elsewhere.[1] For one thing, I don't read Greek or Hebrew, and I don't presume that most readers do either.

---

1. A good book on this topic is *Homoeroticism in the Biblical World* by Martti Nissinen, mainly because, in addition to his scholarly rigor and surprising readability (it's translated from Finnish), Nissinen doesn't seem to have any particular ax to grind. For a good example of a debate between a traditionalist and a non-traditionalist (along with some helpful references to other works), see Gagnon and Via.

Moreover, as an acknowledged religious skeptic, I don't really have a dog in the fight: I'm interested in the Biblical authors' views about same-sex relations primarily for cultural and historical reasons, rather than for uniquely authoritative moral pronouncements. So my goal in this chapter is relatively modest: I want to examine the handful of texts commonly cited against homosexuality and show how the "God said it, I believe it, that settles it" approach is simplistic at best. Even assuming that the Judeo-Christian Bible is God's unerring word, reasonable people may differ on what these texts mean for the topic at hand, not to mention what they mean for secular marriage policy and other political debates. More than anything, this chapter is a plea for humility, directed particularly at those who are inclined to wield the Bible as a moral and political weapon. I focus on the Judeo-Christian Bible because of its dominant place in American culture and its frequent appearance in the gay-rights debate. Except where noted, translations are from the New Revised Standard Version.

Fire and Brimstone

The Sodom and Gomorrah story may be the Biblical passage most often cited against homosexuality. It may also be the least relevant.

This claim surprises many people—after all, the term "sodomy" is etymologically linked to Sodom, a Biblical city destroyed for its wickedness. But equating that wickedness with homosexuality is dubious. We call sodomy "sodomy" because medieval theologians (mis)read Sodom's sin to be same-sex copulation, not because the text itself makes the connection.[2]

---

2. See Jordan, esp. chapter 2, for a detailed scholarly treatment.

A bit of background: Sodom and Gomorrah are sister cities rampant with wickedness, and the Lord intends to destroy them. Abraham urges the Lord to spare the righteous (including, presumably, his nephew Lot), and the Lord sends angels to investigate. After some urging, Lot convinces the angels to spend the night at his home. The city was a frequent passage point for travelers—think of Sodom and Gomorrah as the Minneapolis and St. Paul of the time—and it was common for weary foreigners to camp in the city square. Here's the key passage:

> But [Lot] urged [the visiting angels] strongly; so they turned aside to him and entered his house; and he made them a feast, and baked unleavened bread, and they ate. But before they lay down, the men of the city, the men of Sodom, both young and old, all the people to the last man, surrounded the house; and they called to Lot, "Where are the men who came to you tonight? Bring them out to us, so that we may know them." Lot went out of the door to the men, shut the door after him, and said, "I beg you, my brothers, do not act so wickedly. Look, I have two daughters who have not known a man; let me bring them out to you, and do to them as you please; only do nothing to these men, for they have come under the shelter of my roof." But they replied, "Stand back!" And they said, "This fellow came here as an alien, and he would play the judge! Now we will deal worse with you than with them." Then they pressed hard against the man Lot, and came near the door to break it down. (Genesis 19:3–9)

At this point the visitors reached out and brought Lot in to safety, then struck the mob blind. Then Lot and his family fled the city, and the Lord rained fire and brimstone on it.

What should we make of the Sodom and Gomorrah story? Assuming the townsmen's demand to "know" the visitors is intended sexually, the story describes an attempted gang rape of visiting male angels. Now, call me crazy, but I'm going to go out on a limb here and say that *gang rape is bad*. It is bad, period, regardless of the perpetrators' and victim's genders.

Why, then, is the Sodom story taken as a paradigmatic Biblical condemnation of homosexuality? One might wonder whether I've left out relevant background text, but in fact, nowhere else in the Hebrew Scriptures is Sodom's sin identified as being sexual, much less homosexual. On the contrary, it is explicitly identified as otherwise: "This was the guilt of your sister Sodom: she and her daughters had pride, excess of food, and prosperous ease, but did not aid the poor and needy" (Ezekiel 16:49–50). In other words, the Sodomites were self-indulgent and callous. Not gay.

Sodom's sin is not explicitly identified as sexual until the New Testament. Here's the Epistle of Jude, written at least five centuries after Genesis (and much longer still after the events described):

> Now I desire to remind you, though you are fully informed, that the Lord, who once for all saved a people out of the land of Egypt, afterward destroyed those who did not believe. And the angels who did not keep their own position, but left their proper dwelling, he has kept in eternal chains in deepest darkness for the judgment of the great Day. Likewise, Sodom and Gomorrah and the surrounding cities, which, in the same manner as they, indulged in sexual immorality and pursued unnatural lust, serve as an example by undergoing a punishment of eternal fire (Jude 1:5–7).

While modern readers might be tempted to read "unnatural lust" as a reference to homosexuality, the Greek—literally, "went after other flesh"—more likely refers to the human/angel boundary (as even traditionalist scholars admit).[3] It would be odd to describe the flesh of someone of the same sex as "other flesh"—indeed, the term is more apt for *hetero*sexuality. Biblical authors like to emphasize boundaries, and the human/angel boundary—which we seldom think about, since angels don't typically knock on our doors—was at least as important to them as the male-female one. Notice Jude's reference to the bad angels "who did not keep their own position, but left their proper dwelling." Genesis 6 also discusses how the "Sons of God" (angels) made wives of the "daughters of men." In any case, for authors to say many centuries after the events that Sodom "indulged in sexual immorality and went after other flesh" is vague and inconclusive at best.

Not long ago I explained all this to a Baptist pastor in Kentucky, who gave a common traditionalist response: "But what about Lot's offer of his virgin daughters, which the men rejected? That proves it was about homosexuality!" I always find this response surprising, for a few reasons.

First, Lot's offer of his daughters is an embarrassing detail of the text—*for traditionalists*. Lot is supposed to be the hero of the story, favored by God for his moral character. Even St. Peter in the New Testament repeatedly refers to Lot as a "righteous" man.[4] And when faced with angry rapists, what does a righteous man do? Why, he

---

3. For example, Robert Gagnon, perhaps the most outspoken contemporary biblical opponent of homosexuality, supports this reading of "other flesh," even while he maintains that Sodom's sin is homosexuality. See Gagnon and Via, p. 58. For my own discussion of the relevance of personal experience to Biblical interpretation, see Corvino, 2008.

4. More precisely, *the author of the second epistle of Peter* writes this, at 2 Peter 2:7. Most scholars believe the author to be someone other than St. Peter.

offers them his virgin daughters, of course! If you want an example of how the Bible sometimes portrays women as expendable property, you need look no further than the Sodom and Gomorrah story.

(Quick aside: later in Genesis 19, Lot's daughters get him drunk and become pregnant by him.[5] In response, the Lord—who incidentally had turned Lot's wife into a pillar of salt merely for turning around when she wasn't supposed to—does nothing. I swear, modern reality-TV families look tame by comparison to this clan.)

Now you might respond that Lot was making the best of a bad situation. Or you might argue that, while Lot shouldn't have offered his daughters, God spared him because he was otherwise a pretty good guy. In any case, I haven't yet responded to the pastor's concern: the rapists' turning down Lot's daughters proves that they wanted a man, which proves that God destroyed Sodom for homosexuality.

Consider the bizarre logic behind this position. Suppose that, for example, two blonde females are visiting my house, an angry mob tries to rape them, and I offer them my brunette daughters instead. The mob declines, and God (who was already planning on punishing them anyway) rains fire and brimstone upon them. Surely you wouldn't conclude that *God hates sex with blondes*. Again, rape is very bad and worthy of punishment, regardless of the other particulars.

But there's another important textual detail. If the mob merely wanted another man, they had access to one: "Lot went out of the door to the men [and] shut the door after him." He was standing outside with the door closed. They could have raped him, but they didn't; instead, they continued to press for the strangers. Why?

---

5. Genesis 19:30–38.

To answer that question, consider a very similar story at Judges 19. A Levite priest and his party are offered lodging by an old man while traveling through Gibeah. A mob surrounds the house and demands to "know" the visitors. The old man protests:

> "No, my brothers, do not act so wickedly. Since this man is my guest, do not do this vile thing. Here are my virgin daughter and his concubine; let me bring them out now. Ravish them and do whatever you want to them; but against this man do not do such a vile thing." But the men would not listen to him. So the man seized his concubine, and put her out to them. They wantonly raped her, and abused her all through the night until the morning. (Judges 19: 23–25).

The parallels are striking. Again, we have an ugly mob demanding to "know" visitors, an offer of women (this time, the host's virgin daughter and his guest's concubine), and a refusal of that offer. In this story, however, the concubine is forced out, and the mob repeatedly rapes her. Meanwhile, her master and his host go to sleep. When they awake the next morning, they find her dead at the doorstep.

The rape, of course, is horrid, as is the master's apparent indifference to his concubine's life. But the fact that the mob rapes the concubine (literally to death) suggests that their aim has little to do with same-sex attraction, much less consensual same-sex relationships, and everything to do with abuse. Like the xenophobic mob at Sodom, they seek to humiliate a foreigner by sexually violating him. Frustrated in that goal, they direct their violence elsewhere.

One need not reach into ancient history to find examples of this mindset. Reports of soldiers in the Middle East humiliating captives by stripping, fondling, and sodomizing them are not uncommon even today. In that light, the Biblical mob's attempted rape looks sadly familiar, and citing it to condemn homosexuality is akin to citing the Abu Ghraib prison scandal for the same purpose, just because male-male sexual abuse occurred there (amidst various other crimes).

Some contemporary exegetes—and not only revisionists—suggest that the true sin of Sodom is inhospitality. Without a doubt, Sodom did not treat its visitors well. But "inhospitality" seems a rather weak term for the mistreatment described. Failing to offer your visitors a beverage, after they have traveled a long way to see you, is inhospitality. Trying to gang rape them is quite another matter. (And let's not even talk about offering them your virgin daughters, which apparently is Biblical good form.) Those who seek a compelling Biblical condemnation of consensual homosexuality need to look elsewhere.

Black and White

Let us turn instead to the most explicit and forceful Biblical prohibition of homosexual conduct, which is found in Leviticus:

> "You shall not lie with a male as with a woman; it is an abomination." (18:22)

> "If a man lies with a male as with a woman, both of them have committed an abomination; they shall be put to death; their blood is upon them." (20:13)

Unlike the Sodom and Gomorrah story, these lines seem to require little interpretation. There it is, in black and white: *you shall not lie with a male as with a woman.*

But what does it mean to lie with a male "as with a woman"? Since men and women have different parts, one cannot *literally* lie with one in the same way as with the other. Most likely the text is referring to male-male anal sex, the closest approximation to sex "as with a woman." Prohibiting such activity makes sense given ancient Hebrew notions of male superiority: according to their view, to treat a man as a woman—in this case, to sexually penetrate him—would be to degrade him: women have their place, and that place is (literally and figuratively) "beneath" men.[6] That same attitude explains why Lot and the Gibean man view the rape of male guests as far worse than that of their own daughters.

Notice a few things. First, neither this text nor anything else in the Hebrew Scriptures mentions lesbian sex. One might suspect that this oversight reflects a more general lack of attention to women, but elsewhere the Leviticus authors explicitly prohibit both male and female bestiality, so it is not as if women's sexual activity is entirely an afterthought for them. Notice, too, that the interpretation just offered says nothing about other forms of romantic interaction between men besides anal intercourse. One might naturally take "as with a woman" to refer to *any* romantic or sexual activity, but reading it that way supplies information that is not explicitly in the text. It requires interpretation and thus introduces human fallibility.

It may seem that I'm splitting hairs here. And for the record, I am not suggesting the Leviticus authors would be keen on male-male oral sex, mutual masturbation, romantic kissing, and so on. Many years ago, an audience member at one of my talks asked me, "What would you say to gay men who believe that Levitical law is binding?"

---

6. See Nissinen, 128–31 and elsewhere.

My too-flippant answer, which I'm embarrassed now to admit, was "Not much": I think the most plausible reading of Leviticus 18:22 is "No male-male sex, period," and unlike loophole-seeking teenagers, I think oral sex is sex. Because of the stage lights and the questioner's distance, I didn't notice at the time that he was wearing a kippah (yarmulke): I later learned that he was a gay Orthodox Jew who genuinely struggled with the question. (We have since become friends.)

For those of us who are not Orthodox Jews, Levitical law is interesting historically but not terribly informative morally. After all, it proclaims that eating shellfish is "detestable," it forbids wearing clothing of mixed fibers, and it condemns eating the flesh or touching the carcass of a cloven-hoofed animal (such as a pig), declaring such activities "unclean."[7] It's possible that those laws had a good rationale then, but no longer do. But it is also possible that the same is true for the prohibition of male-male penetration.

The selective (mis)use of Hebrew Scriptures in the gay-rights debate has been noted and satirized frequently. Consider, for instance, the following internet gem: a purported open letter to "Dr. Laura," a conservative radio talk-show host:

Dear Dr. Laura,

Thank you for doing so much to educate people regarding God's Law. I have learned a great deal from your show, and I try to share that knowledge with as many people as I can. When

---

7. For shellfish, see Leviticus 11: 10–12. (The King James Version actually uses the word "abomination" here.) For fibers, see Leviticus 19:19. For cloven-hoofed animals, see Leviticus 11:8.

someone tries to defend the homosexual lifestyle, for example, I simply remind him that Leviticus 18:22 clearly states it to be an abomination. End of debate.

I do need some advice from you, however, regarding some of the specific laws and how to best follow them.

(a) When I burn a bull on the altar as a sacrifice, I know it creates a pleasing odor for the Lord (Lev. 1:9). The problem is my neighbors. They claim the odor is not pleasing to them. Should I smite them?

(b) I would like to sell my daughter into slavery, as sanctioned in Exodus 21:7. In this day and age, what do you think would be a fair price for her?

(c) I know that I am allowed no contact with a woman while she is in her period of menstrual uncleanliness (Lev. 15:19–24). The problem is, how do I tell? I have tried asking, but most women take offense.

(d) Lev. 25:44 states that I may indeed possess slaves, both male and female, provided they are purchased from neighboring nations. A friend of mine claims that this applies to Mexicans, but not Canadians. Can you clarify? Why can't I own Canadians?

(e) I have a neighbor who insists on working on the Sabbath. Exodus 35:2 clearly states he should be put to death. Am I morally obligated to kill him myself?

(f) A friend of mine feels that even though eating shellfish is an abomination (Lev. 11:10), it is a lesser abomination than homosexuality. I don't agree. Can you settle this?

(g) Lev. 21:20 states that I may not approach the altar of God if I have a defect in my sight. I have to admit that I wear reading glasses. Does my vision have to be 20/20, or is there some wiggle room here?

(h) Most of my male friends get their hair trimmed, including the hair around their temples, even though this is expressly forbidden by Lev. 19:27. How should they die?

(i) I know from Lev. 11:6–8 that touching the skin of a dead pig makes me unclean, but may I still play football if I wear gloves?

(j) My uncle has a farm. He violates Lev. 19:19 by planting two different crops in the same field, as does his wife by wearing garments made of two different kinds of thread (cotton/polyester blend). He also tends to curse and blaspheme a lot. Is it really necessary that we go to all the trouble of getting the whole town together to stone them? (Lev. 24:10–16) Couldn't we just burn them to death at a private family affair like we do with people who sleep with their in-laws? (Lev. 20:14)

I know you have studied these things extensively, so I am confident you can help. Thank you again for reminding us that God's word is eternal and unchanging.

Christians will often claim that the dietary laws and such are dispensed with in the New Testament, so they don't apply anymore. The main problem with this response is that it largely misses the point. Even if the New Testament somehow "overrides" the Old Testament—like one of those "change of terms" notices credit card companies periodically send—Leviticus is still supposed to be *God's word*. Yet when one reads it in its entirety, it's hard to avoid the sense that this book contains not, in fact, the unerring word of an all-good, all-knowing, all-powerful God, but instead the occasionally reasonable but often flawed rules of fallible human beings, rules that are intricately bound to the authors' cultural circumstances. For instance, God's alleged word here tells us that it is okay to make slaves of people, and for our children to inherit them as property (Leviticus 25:44–46). Leviticus makes—to borrow Tammy's word—*mistakes*, including serious moral mistakes. But once you make that concession, you can no longer use "the Bible says so" as a moral trump card.

Some traditionalists would object that I have overlooked the most important "Old Testament" passage in this debate: the creation account, where God creates humanity male and female:

> So God created humankind in his image, in the image of God he created them; male and female he created them. God blessed them, and God said to them, "Be fruitful and multiply, and fill the earth and subdue it . . ." (Genesis 1:27–28).

To put the argument in more popular terms, "It's Adam and Eve, not Adam and Steve."

There is no doubt that Genesis (and indeed, the Bible more generally) endorses a male-female paradigm for sexuality. But it is important not to read too much into this fact, or to draw nonsequiturs from it. From the fact that God tells these early humans to "fill the earth and subdue it," it does not follow that *every* human being must procreate (St. Paul, for example, did not). Nor does it follow that no one may ever engage in intentionally non-procreative sex. And from the fact that God labels one thing as *good*, it does not follow that other things are *bad*.

To be fair, I should mention that pro-gay Christians indulge in similar nonsequiturs, such as when they point out that Jesus never says anything about homosexuality and conclude that his silence must indicate approval. Well, Jesus didn't say anything about abolishing slavery, either. It's always dangerous to read too much into what the Bible *doesn't* say.

Genesis was written as a narrative, not a rulebook. The authors aim to describe creation (whether literally or metaphorically), including facts about men and women and the relationships they tend to form: "Therefore a man leaves his father and his mother and clings to his wife, and they become one flesh" (2:24). One must be careful when seeking more general normative guidelines from narratives, for there is a fine line between reading a message *from* the text and reading one *into* the text. The creation narrative, in particular, often gets treated as a kind of inkblot test: People see there what they want to see, like, "No gay sex," or "You're my wife; defer to me," or "Of course I can treat animals however I want."

It's even possible to find gay-friendly messages in the creation stories, especially the second one. (There are two consecutive creation stories in Genesis, with the second beginning around 2:5, and they're technically inconsistent.) There God says, "It is not good that the man should be alone; I will make him a helper as his partner" (2:18). God then presents Adam with various animals and birds, all of which Adam finds unsuitable. It is not until God presents Adam with Woman, whom he creates from Adam's rib, that Adam is satisfied. The overarching theme appears to be *companionship*, and it's noteworthy that God doesn't simply make an executive decision about which creature will be suitable: he brings them to Adam and lets him choose. The implication is that individuals—including, presumably, gays and lesbians—are the experts on their own hearts.

Does this pro-gay interpretation read too much into Genesis? Perhaps. But it does so no more than the "no gay sex" interpretation does.

Out with the Old, in with the New

Over my years debating same-sex marriage, I've noticed that although many people oppose homosexuality on Biblical grounds, few will publicly debate the following specific question: "Should society adopt a Biblical view of marriage?" Once, in an unguarded, off-camera moment, I asked a prominent evangelical why.

"That's easy," he answered. "It's because of all that crazy Old Testament stuff." I was surprised by his honesty but not by his answer. The Old Testament can be pretty hard to swallow. It has concubines and slaves and a bunch of weird rules. It often portrays God as an angry and jealous bully, who plays favorites and changes his mind a lot. It's no wonder that Christians prefer to focus on the kinder, gentler New Testament.

Like the Old Testament, the New Testament contains some difficult-to-translate passages. You don't need to read ancient Greek or Aramaic to realize this. You just need to observe the various ways that different scholars have rendered the same passage.

Take, for example, Paul's First Letter to the Corinthians 6:9–10. (A very similar passage appears at I Timothy 1:9–10). The widely respected New Revised Standard Version translates the passage as follows:

> Do you not know that wrongdoers will not inherit the kingdom
> of God? Do not be deceived! Fornicators, idolaters, adulterers,
> male prostitutes, sodomites, thieves, the greedy, drunkards, revilers, robbers—none of these will inherit the kingdom of God.

The difficult term here is *arsenokoitai*, rendered here as "sodomites." What does it mean? No one knows for sure. It's a compound term made up of the Greek words for male (*arsen*) and bed (*koite*), but there's no record of it before Paul, and it's quite likely that he made it up. Translators have thus had to guess at its meaning, and their guesses have been various:

King James Version (1611): "neither fornicators, nor idolaters, nor adulterers, nor effeminate, nor *abusers of themselves with mankind* ..."

American Standard Version (1901): "neither fornicators, nor idolaters, nor adulterers, nor effeminate, nor *abusers of themselves with men* ..."

Revised Standard Version (1946): "neither the immoral, nor idolaters, nor adulterers, nor *sexual perverts* ..."

New American Standard (1963): "neither fornicators, nor idolaters, nor adulterers, nor effeminate, nor *homosexuals* ..."

Good News Bible (1966): "people who are immoral or who worship idols or are adulterers or *homosexual perverts* ..."

New American Bible (1970): "neither fornicators nor idolaters nor adulterers nor boy prostitutes nor *sodomites* ..."

New International Version (1973): "neither the sexually immoral nor idolaters nor adulterers nor male prostitutes nor *homosexual offenders* ..."

New Revised Standard Version (1989): "fornicators, idolaters, adulterers, male prostitutes, *sodomites* ..."

Put aside the fact that the claim about "fornicators" would damn many of the same people who so readily cite the passage against homosexuality. Looking at these translations chronologically, we go from the relatively vague "abusers of themselves with men," to the even vaguer "sexual perverts," to the much more specific "homosexuals," then "homosexual perverts," then "sodomites" (alongside the unique "boy prostitutes"), then "homosexual offenders," then back to "sodomites." In English, the word "sodomite" refers to anyone, heterosexual or homosexual, who engages in sodomy—another vague term. (It can refer variously to anal sex, oral sex, bestiality, or "any of various forms of sexual intercourse held to be unnatural or abnormal," according to the *American Heritage Dictionary*.)

I repeat: no one knows for sure what *arsenokoitai* means.

Given its root elements ("male" and "bed"), it almost surely refers to something men do sexually. Given its proximity to *malakoi* (literally, "soft")—rendered here variously as "effeminate," "boy prostitutes," "male prostitutes" and so on—it might refer to men who procure such prostitutes' services. (Male prostitution was a familiar part of pagan temple worship during Biblical times.) It is also possible that Paul is trying to echo the Hebrew Scriptures as rendered in the Septuagint, a Greek translation familiar at the time: Leviticus 18:22 and 20:13 prohibit the male (*arsen*) from lying with (*koiten*) a male as with a woman. But any interpretation will be somewhat speculative, and we should perhaps admire scholars who admit their uncertainty by choosing vague translations like "sexual perverts," in contrast to the overconfident "God said it" crowd.

Romans and Revisionism

Revisionists often seize upon these problems to argue that the Bible opposes not same-sex relations across-the-board, but rather specific homosexual practices familiar during Biblical times—for example, pagan temple-prostitution. The idea is that even though the prohibitions are not put forth in such a way as to limit them to specific homosexual practices, those are the practices the Biblical authors likely had in mind, given that they were the primary models of homosexuality available. This revisionist idea also responds to those who note the Bible's "consistent witness" against homosexuality—the fact that every time it mentions same-sex relations the tone is negative: This negativity may well be explained by the models of homosexuality the authors focused on. Besides, most of the allegedly relevant passages occur in contexts where the authors contrast the chosen people's behavior with that of pagans—suggesting that idolatry, not homosexuality, may be their real target.

A good example is Paul's Epistle to the Romans, which many consider to contain the most substantial Christian Biblical reference to homosexuality. Early in the letter, Paul writes about non-Jews who "exchanged the glory of the immortal god" for the worship of graven images: birds, reptiles, and such. Their idolatry causes God to hand them over to sexual shamelessness:

> For this reason [idolatry] God gave them up to degrading passions. Their women exchanged natural intercourse for unnatural, and in the same way also the men, giving up natural intercourse with women, were consumed with passion for one another. Men committed shameless acts with men and received in their own persons the due penalty for their error (1:26–27).

Revisionists give different analyses of this text. Some argue that Paul's use of "unnatural" (*para physin*, "against nature") refers to the unconventional rather than the immoral, since the Bible says that even God sometimes acts *para physin*. Certainly, we should be careful of reading too much modern meaning into the term: the Roman philosopher Seneca taught that hot baths, potted plants, and banquets after sunset were all "against nature," and Paul makes a similar claim about men who wear their hair long.[8] "Seriously unconventional" might be a less misleading, albeit less literal, translation of *para physin*.

Other revisionists argue that Paul's wording suggests concern with heterosexuals who practice homosexuality—they "exchanged" natural intercourse for unnatural—and so the passage doesn't apply to those whose "natural" orientation is homosexual. Paul, like his contemporaries, does not seem aware of the possibility of a genuinely homosexual orientation, and he is thus likely to view homosexual conduct as necessarily involving lust, never love.

But the key revisionist insight is as follows: Paul is here addressing a specific group of people (first-century Romans) about a specific group of people (Gentiles who engaged in idolatry). He claims that these Gentiles' same-sex passion is both a sign and consequence of their rejecting Yahweh, the one true God. To read that claim as a blanket statement about *all* homosexual acts is to read too much into the text.

The revisionists do have a point. For if we read Paul as making a general claim, rather than a specific historical commentary, his claim is implausible: There are plenty of people who love Yahweh—indeed, who are devout, Bible-fearing believers—yet who experience same-sex desire. And there are plenty of people who reject Yahweh yet experience no same-sex desire. If Paul were making a general claim about homosexuality, then he would be asserting a causal connection between homosexuality and idolatry for which there is no evidence and much counterevidence.

---

8. 1 Corinthians 11:14–5. For Seneca, see Nissinen, 105.

That said, it's quite likely that Paul would have objected to other forms of homosexuality, including our everyday, nonidolatrous kind. Paul has a negative view of sex generally: he recommends marriage only as a concession to those who cannot personally handle celibacy.[9] His writing, like any author's, often reflects his cultural prejudices and limitations. Two examples will make this point stark.

First, consider what Paul says regarding the role of women in churches: "As in all the churches of the saints, women should be silent in the churches. For they are not permitted to speak, but should be subordinate, as the law also says. If there is anything they desire to know, let them ask their husbands at home. For it is shameful for a woman to speak in church" (1 Corinthians 14:33–35).

Few Christians read this passage to mean what it plainly and explicitly says: *women may not speak in church.* Those who do read it plainly often simply ignore it. Asked to explain, they will usually say something about "cultural differences" and "pulling the passage out of context." In other words, they decline to take the claim as a generally applicable command, even though nothing in the immediate text indicates that Paul intended it more narrowly.

Second, consider Paul's instruction to slaves: "Slaves, obey your earthly masters with fear and trembling, in singleness of heart, as you obey Christ; not only while being watched, and in order to please them, but as slaves of Christ, doing the will of God from the heart" (Ephesians 6:5–6).

Taken generally, the command prohibits slaves from trying to escape—which is exactly how 19th-century American slave-owners read it. It is by no means clear that Paul would have objected to his words being so used. Like his Biblical contemporaries, Paul accepted

---

9. 1 Corinthians 7:1–2.

slavery as a matter of course: He even sends the escaped slave Onesimus back to Philemon (although he also, quite radically, exhorts Philemon to welcome Onesimus as a brother in Christ).[10] Elsewhere Paul writes that in Christ there "is no longer Jew or Greek, there is no longer slave or free, there is no longer male and female" (Galatians 3:28), but one presumes that he intends that as a point about eternal salvation, not as a rejection of earthly distinctions. Indeed, if one reads the claim literally and rejects the earthly distinction of male/female, homosexuality becomes a nonissue.

Paul's acceptance of slavery has strong Biblical footing. Scripture portrays God himself as endorsing slavery. The Lord God says:

> As for the male and female slaves whom you may have, it is from the nations around you that you may acquire male and female slaves. You may also acquire them from among the aliens residing with you, and from their families that are with you, who have been born in your land; and they may be your property. You may keep them as a possession for your children after you, for them to inherit as property. These you may treat as slaves, but as for your fellow Israelites, no one shall rule over the other with harshness. (Leviticus 25:44–46)

The passage makes clear that the word "slaves" really does mean "slaves"—these are not employees, unless you think employees may be inherited "as property." The last sentence even suggests that slaves, unlike fellow Israelites, may be ruled over "with harshness."

It's interesting to watch the interpretative maneuvers people employ to deny that the Bible really endorses slavery. Some point

---

10. See Paul's Epistle to Philemon.

out the Biblical commandment to release slaves every Jubilee year. But this only applies to Israelite slaves, not foreign ones, and it only happens every fifty years. Some fundamentalists also claim that God didn't want slavery but acceded to it because of the hardness of human hearts. But this makes God seem like a wimp: after all, the God of the Bible usually gets what he wants, even if he has to destroy entire cities in the process. Moreover, if God could be swayed by cultural prejudices on slavery, why not by cultural prejudices on homosexuality?

Others argue that Biblical slavery isn't really so bad because God sometimes commands masters not to treat slaves with excessive harshness—although textual support for the latter claim is underwhelming, to say the least. For example: "When a slave-owner strikes a male or female slave with a rod and the slave dies immediately, the owner shall be punished. But if the slave survives for a day or two, there is no punishment; for the slave is the owner's property" (Exodus 21:20–22).

When all that fails, believers will make a plea for looking at the larger message of the Bible, especially the Gospels, and not drawing conclusions about slavery based on a handful of texts yanked out of their historical context. To which I respond . . . Amen. Precisely. But if it's wrong to do that with the slavery passages, why is it okay to do that with the homosexuality passages? Why not, instead, emphasize the Gospel message of love, kindness, and humility in approaching both issues? As I've often said, if the religious right's volume on the "love thy neighbor" message were even half as loud as its volume on the "no gay sex" message, the world would be a much better place.

My point is this: If you adopt a simplistic "God said it" approach to the text, then be prepared to swallow some pretty nasty conclusions about slavery, women, and so on. If, instead, you insist on sensitivity to historical and cultural context, then the homosexuality passages must be reexamined in that light. Loving, mutual, noni-dolatrous same-sex unions are simply not on the Biblical authors' radar, much less the target of these texts. In fact, the main topic of Paul's letter to the Romans is justification by faith, and it includes a sharp condemnation of hypocrisy—which makes it all the more ironic that Christians use Romans 1 as a "clobber passage." Quoting it to condemn contemporary same-sex unions is akin to citing Leviticus 25 or Ephesians 6 to support 19th-century American slavery. If we shouldn't do it in the one case, we shouldn't do it in the other.

Divorce is another analogy worth mentioning at least briefly. According to the Bible, Jesus himself said that "Whoever divorces his wife and marries another commits adultery against her; and if she divorces her husband and marries another, she commits adultery" (Mark 10:11-12). Adultery is a violation of the Ten Commandments, punishable by death in the Old Testament. Yet fundamentalists take a rather different attitude toward, say, the thrice married Newt Gingrich or the four-times married Rush Limbaugh than they do toward gays and lesbians—even though all of the above are unrepentant sinners according to traditional interpretations. (It's not enough to simply "regret" the divorce: the Bible makes it clear that continuing with your current spouse makes you a persistent adulterer.) What this disparity suggests is that people are willing to subject the gay and lesbian minority to a rather different standard of Biblical literalism than they themselves would tolerate.

Mistakes, Again

My own personal view is that whether or not revisionism works for the homosexuality passages (or for that matter, the divorce passages), it's untenable for the slavery passages. It seems pretty clear that the Bible endorses slavery, and the Bible is just wrong about that. But once we admit that the Bible reflects the mistaken cultural prejudices about slavery, we must concede that it may also reflect mistaken cultural prejudices about other things, homosexuality included. Either it's infallible, or it isn't.

From personal experience I know that it can be difficult, at a deeply visceral level, to acknowledge mistakes in the Bible. I grew up a devout Roman Catholic, and I was once even a candidate for the priesthood. I took the Bible very seriously as the word of God. I always noticed that parts of it seemed strange, but like most believers I tended to glide over those. It wasn't until I began studying it carefully—as a philosophy and theology student in college—that I seriously questioned whether the Bible might contain errors. Admitting its fallibility required me to rethink various other core beliefs, and that was a hard (though ultimately healthy) process. Sacred cows don't tip easily.

Some fundamentalists claim that without the Bible, one can have no secure foundation for moral claims. It seems to me that quite the reverse is true: Without an independent moral sense, one can have no confidence that a given text is God's word. After all, many different and incompatible texts claim to be divinely inspired, one cannot sift the good from the bad (or, at least, the better from the worse) without invoking an independent standard. It doesn't follow that the standard is "above" God—remember, believers hold that God is the creator of *everything*. I recall a Christian friend of mine who once wrote me a long letter trying to "save" me from homosexuality. "We trust our own fallible minds," she lamented, "but we do not trust the infallible mind of Christ!" But whose mind do I use to do the trusting, if not my own fallible one? Again, belief in an infallible God does not make the believer infallible.

I also suspect that, despite surface appearances to the contrary, it is relatively uncommon for people to derive their beliefs about same-sex relationships from the Bible. It is far more common for them to seek Biblical backing for things they already believe independently. (To be fair, both sides do this.) Add to this the fact that people on both sides sincerely believe that God speaks to them in prayer—with contradictory messages—and you can see why it's important, especially in our religiously diverse society, for participants in this debate to offer secular reasons which are in principle accessible to all.

None of this settles the moral status of homosexuality. It simply means that we must look beyond "the Bible says so" to settle it. And so let us now turn to some secular arguments.

3 | "A RISKY LIFESTYLE"

Several years ago I was invited to contribute a chapter on homosexuality to a point/counterpoint book on social issues. Christopher Wolfe, a political scientist who was then at Marquette University, would be my opponent, and we agreed to share drafts during the writing process. These began with the usual pleasantries—"I am delighted by the opportunity for this exchange with Professor So-and-So"—proceeded through several rounds of revisions; and ended, as such things often do, with a series of irritated footnotes—"Professor So-and-So is just being obtuse if he can't see how wrong he is here."

Neither one of us actually used the word "obtuse," although I imagine we were both thinking it. In hindsight, I suppose I started the snarkiness. Focusing my chapter on homosexuality's alleged harms, I used Wolfe's earlier essay "Homosexuality in American Public Life" as a foil. There Wolfe notes some "very substantial costs that are often, though not always, associated with living as a homosexual," including "a very dramatic decrease in life expectancy—in some studies, for male homosexuals, on the order of twenty-five to thirty years," various diseases, higher rates of suicide, and so on. He then asked:

On the basis of health considerations alone, is it unreasonable to ask if it is better not to be an active homosexual? At the very least, don't the facts suggest that it is desirable to prevent the formation of a homosexual orientation and to bring people out of it when we can?[1]

After quoting these lines in my contribution, I offered the admittedly cheeky retort, "The trouble with rhetorical questions is that people sometimes answer them." (The retort must have stung its target, since Wolfe used the same wording against me in a footnote later on.)

Still, fair is fair. If you're going to paint the "homosexual lifestyle" as a cesspool of disease and despair, I'm going to strike back hard. Because when you're talking about that "lifestyle," you're talking about my life, and in particular, my life with Mark. Descriptions of homosexual misery ring false to me.

Portraying homosexuality as catastrophic is nothing new. The ancient Roman Emperor Justinian blamed it for earthquakes, plagues, famine, and various other maladies. Modern-day critics have been only slightly less creative, citing gays for the breakdown of the family, the AIDS crisis, sexual abuse scandals—even the 9/11 attacks. Here's the late Jerry Falwell, speaking on Pat Robertson's Christian television show *The 700 Club* in the wake of that atrocity: "I really believe that the pagans, and the abortionists, and the feminists, and the gays and the lesbians who are actively trying to make that an alternative lifestyle, the ACLU, People For the American Way, all of them who have tried to secularize America. I point the finger in their face and say 'you helped this happen.'" Falwell later issued a half-hearted apology, but by then the damage was done—to his reputation. At a time of such national mourning, not even his friends could stomach such blatant and ugly scapegoating.

The Reverend Jerry Falwell speaking on *The 700 Club* is one thing, but Professor Christopher Wolfe writing in a respectable

---

1. Wolfe 2000, p. 12.

academic anthology is another. And he's not alone. Harm arguments constitute one of the two major strands of secular arguments against homosexuality. (The other is natural law arguments, which I'll cover in the next chapter.) In the debate over same-sex marriage, for example, many people allege harm to the traditional family and particularly to children; in the (now seemingly settled) debate over gays in the military, many alleged harm to combat effectiveness, and so on. Scripture scholar Robert Gagnon, a frequent commentator on homosexuality, often mentions "disproportionately high rates of measurable harm" when making his secular case. Invoking statistics and other empirical data, such arguments can have a compelling scientific ring. And they're based on an unassailable premise: all else being equal, it's bad to hurt oneself or others.

That's why Wolfe's question seems so reasonable, and even compassionate, on the surface: on the basis of health considerations alone, shouldn't we try to discourage homosexuality? And that's why it's tempting for those who believe Wolfe's disease statistics to answer "yes." But the correct answer, even if we assume the statistics to be accurate (which they are not) isn't so simple. It depends on the answers to a number of other questions, none of which Wolfe—or most opponents of homosexuality—bother to ask very carefully. In this chapter I'll explore those questions.

The First Question: Are the Allegations of Harm Accurate?

This question is elementary but crucial. When studying human behavior, it is difficult to isolate relevant factors from other influences. The study of sexuality is especially challenging, since shyness, fear, and the powerful phenomenon of the closet make it notoriously difficult to get adequate representative samples. Even in today's more "accepting" climate, many gay and lesbian people are not prepared to come out to themselves, much less to researchers. This fact complicates an already complicated endeavor.

Of course, some studies are better than others. The problem is that most studies cited by gay-rights opponents are abysmally bad. Consider Wolfe's claim, taken from Jeffrey Satinover, that homosexuals suffer "a very dramatic decrease in life expectancy—in some studies, for male homosexuals, on the order of twenty-five to thirty years."[2] Satinover supports this jarring statistic by citing a 1993 paper, "The Homosexual Lifespan."[3] In their study, psychologist Paul Cameron and his colleagues argued that the average lifespan for gay males was between 39 years of age (for those who die of AIDS-related causes) and 42 years of age (for those who die of other causes). In other words, they claimed that *even apart from AIDS*, gay men on average die over 30 years sooner than their straight counterparts.

How did they reach this startling conclusion? By comparing obituaries in 16 gay publications with those in two mainstream newspapers.

Just to be clear: I am not making this up. The methodology in this study is laughable even to those with no formal training in statistics. First, newspaper obituaries, which are typically written by relatives, hardly constitute a reliable scientific source. Second, obituaries that appeared in gay publications during the 1980s were not likely to be representative of the gay community at large, both because of their target demographic and because older gays

---

2. Cited in Wolfe 2000, p. 12.

3. Presentation to the Eastern Psychological Association, April 1993. Later published as Cameron, 1994.

were (and still are) more likely to be closeted. Remember that obituaries are submitted by survivors, and the survivors of elderly gays are often their heterosexual nieces and nephews—not your typical *Advocate* subscribers. Third, there was no genuine control group: gay people have obituaries in mainstream publications too, and unless a partner or "longtime companion" is mentioned, these are often indistinguishable from those of straight people. Fourth, and perhaps most bizarrely, the study included no *living* people. (It should go without saying, but one cannot do a comparative study of life expectancy without recording the ages of the living.) And so on. It should come as no surprise that a decade earlier Cameron was expelled from the American Psychological Association for "a violation of the Preamble to the Ethical Principles of Psychologists."[4] He was later condemned by the Nebraska Psychological Association and the American Sociological Association for his misrepresentations of scientific research on sexuality.[5]

Even Satinover, from whom Wolfe cited the data, had reservations about Cameron: "Because of the researcher's rough and ready methodology, these findings must be considered preliminary."[6] Rough and ready? Preliminary? Try useless.

Actually, "useless" isn't quite right. Paul Cameron's "research" continues to be useful to those who want to paint a certain picture of gay life regardless of the facts. It is also useful for another reason.

---

4. Letter from the American Psychological Association to Paul Cameron, December 2, 1983. Cameron has since circulated the letter and claimed that he had resigned prior to its issuance. But APA rules prohibit members from resigning while under investigation.

5. "Minutes of the Nebraska Psychological Association," October 19, 1984, and *ASA Footnotes*, Feb. 1987, p. 14.

6. Cited in Wolfe 2000, p. 12.

As Dr. Morton Frisch, senior epidemiologist at Copenhagen's Statens Serum Institut, put it (discussing a similar study by Cameron and Cameron's son on Danish gay life expectancy): "Although the Camerons' report has no objective scientific value, the authors should be acknowledged for providing teachers with a humorous example of agenda-driven, pseudo-scientific gobbledygook that will make lessons in elementary study design and scientific inference much more amusing for future epidemiology students."[7]

Why worry about a charlatan like Cameron? Because he continues to get cited by serious scholars like Wolfe and Gagnon. In this manner, bizarre myths about gays get passed around as serious research.

I included these criticisms in my response to Wolfe. He replied in a footnote:

> But, even if [Corvino's] critique of one study is correct, that would only leave us without any evidence one way or the other on the allegations of the dangers, because he has given us no empirical evidence at all on the other side (i.e., that heterosexual and homosexual longevity is similar). The question of danger would remain, therefore, simply an open question.[8]

Now, it seems to me that if someone cites an embarrassingly bad study as his evidence for a shocking claim and then gets called out on it, the burden of proof is on him to reestablish the claim if he so desires. Calling the claim an "open question" at this point is akin to calling Barack Obama's alleged foreign birth an open question after

---

7. http://wthrockmorton.com/2007/04/13/only-the-gay-die-young-part-2-danish-epidemiologist-reviews-the-cameron-study/.

8. Wolfe 2007, p. 106.

discrediting "research" aiming to prove it: there's just no reason to believe the claim otherwise, and plenty of reason to suspect a myth. And it's not as if I picked a laughable study for the sake of inventing a straw man: I picked the study that Wolfe himself—a tenured professor at a respected university—cited as his main evidence.

Wolfe's footnote continues: "In fact, however, the (concededly problematic) conclusions of the Cameron study received qualified support from another (less controversial) study that estimates that life expectancy for gay males is 8–20 years less than for all men."[9] This latter study, by Hogg et al., is indeed less controversial. But now Wolfe is being either disingenuous or sloppy (although I appreciate the "concededly problematic").

Hogg's study is entitled "Modeling the Impact of HIV Disease on Mortality in Gay and Bisexual Men," and it studies (not surprisingly) the impact of HIV disease on mortality in gay and bisexual men, in Vancouver from 1987 to 1992. It is no secret that, in urban centers from 1987 and 1992, many gay men died very young because of HIV. But by the time Wolfe wrote his contribution (around 2006), educational and especially medical advances had reduced the incidence of HIV-related deaths dramatically, both for men who have sex with men and for the population at large. To use the relatively narrow Hogg study to support the blanket conclusion that "life expectancy for gay males is 8–20 years less than for all men" seems pretty desperate at this point.

But don't take my word for it. Take Hogg's: In a 2001 letter to the journal that published his study, he condemned its use "to suggest that gay and bisexual men live an unhealthy lifestyle that is destructive to themselves and to others" and stated that his results

---

9. Citing Hogg et al. 1997.

would no longer hold up even for the narrow population he had considered.[10] Much more recently, the *Journal of the American Medical Association* reported that mortality rates for HIV-infected persons in developed nations have become much closer to general mortality rates since the introduction of new therapies.[11]

What does the best available current research say about the life expectancy of gay or bisexual men? The truth is that there is scant research addressing this question in a general way, rather than looking at a more specific issue, such as AIDS in urban centers or suicide among gay youth. And there's hardly anything at all on lesbians. Wolfe's allegation about homosexual life expectancy remains essentially baseless.

There's another problem with Wolfe's rejoinder here. Wolfe claims that even if my critique of Cameron "is correct, that would only leave us without any evidence one way or the other on the allegations of the dangers." That's true as far as it goes. Indeed, I conceded as much in my paper, where I wrote, "Of course, discrediting Cameron's obituary studies is not tantamount to discrediting the right-wing's entire case (though, frankly, it does not help their credibility). So let me shift gears a bit. Suppose, *purely for the sake of argument*, we were to grant the allegations of harm cited by gay-rights opponents."[12]

The problem is that Wolfe just ignores this step in the argument. My overall argument against Wolfe was a layered one, where no step required accepting the previous layer. Step one: Rebut Wolfe's central evidence about the dangers of the homosexual lifestyle. Step

---

10. Hogg 2001.

11. Bhaskaran et al.

12. Corvino 2007, p. 83.

two: Argue that, even if Wolfe were right about the dangers, it doesn't automatically follow that homosexuality should be discouraged. Why? Because we still need to ask another question.

The Second Question: Are the Alleged Harms Caused by Homosexuality Itself, or Some Extrinsic Factor?

The focus on AIDS makes it pretty easy to demonstrate this problem: gay sex doesn't kill people, AIDS does. And if the HIV virus isn't present, people can have as much gay sex as they like without worrying about AIDS. (Fatigue, yes; AIDS, no.)

But of course this answer is too easy. (Much like "Guns don't kill people . . .") Wolfe would doubtless respond that, for men, sex with men is statistically more likely to transmit the HIV virus than sex with women. As a general matter this claim is true (given various significant qualifications), but it is unclear what follows. Consider the fact that, for women, heterosexual sex is statistically more likely to transmit the HIV virus than homosexual sex. (One could make a similar argument from the premise that, prior to modern medicine, childbirth could be quite risky for any woman.) Yet no one concludes that the Surgeon General ought to recommend lesbianism, or that, on the basis of health considerations alone, female heterosexuality should be discouraged. There are simply too many missing steps.

AIDS is associated with homosexuality in this country because gay men were the population hit first, and hardest, by the disease. But it bears repeating that gay sex, like straight sex, can happen in many different ways (different positions, occasions, partners, and so on) and that many of them place people at relatively low risk of AIDS. So even if Wolfe's data were accurate, it would not be *homosexuality* we should discourage on the basis of health consider-ations, but risky sexual practices, including any sex (heterosexual or homosexual) involving a partner of unknown or positive HIV-status ejaculating into another.

As a gay man who is HIV-negative and doesn't engage in prac-tices that would put me at any significant risk for contracting HIV, I find the right wing's obsessive focus on AIDS and other sexually transmitted diseases tiresome. I have a greater risk of being hit by a runaway school bus than of developing AIDS. So given the choice between staying home to have sex with my HIV-negative partner and leaving the house to do anything, it's probably safer for me to stay home and have sex. (With my luck, I'll die hitting my head on the headboard, and my opponents will gloat "Aha!") AIDS doesn't just "happen" in gay sex as a matter of course: The virus must be present. No virus, no AIDS risk.

AIDS is not the only case where opponents display a "blame the victim" mentality. Consider Wolfe's inclusion of "higher rates of suicide" among his reasons for opposing homosexuality. This item is surprising, given that the most plausible explanation for such rates is anti-gay sentiment and the resulting isolation, particularly among gay and lesbian youth. A recent study in the journal *Pediatrics* re-ports that "lesbian, gay, and bisexual young adults who reported higher levels of family rejection during adolescence were 8.4 times more likely to report having attempted suicide, 5.9 times more likely to report high levels of depression, 3.4 times more likely to use ille-gal drugs, and 3.4 times more likely to report having engaged in un-protected sexual intercourse compared with peers from families that reported no or low levels of family rejection."[13] Here we have a

---

13. Ryan et al.

vicious circle: Opponents of homosexuality base their opposition on factors caused by that very opposition—in other words, blaming the victim. It's like the bully on the playground who teases his classmate, causing him to cry, and then justifies the teasing on the grounds that his classmate is a crybaby.

Of course, the extrinsic explanations for the dangers aren't always so easy or straightforward. Take the alleged promiscuity of gays (not itself usually categorized as a harm, strictly speaking, but sometimes correlated with harms). Michael Levin, a philosopher at the City University of New York and another prominent critic of homosexuality, has offered the following argument against extrinsic explanations for gay promiscuity:

> Liberationists explain the promiscuity of homosexuals by the forbidden nature of their love. Taboo desires naturally result in furtive, sordid encounters, they say; were homosexuality accepted and homosexual marriage permitted, homosexuals would be as faithful as heterosexuals. But this explanation has worn thin. The intelligentsia and the media have been pro-homosexual for three decades. Can you recall the last homosexual portrayed unsympathetically in the movies or on TV? The love that dare not speak its name is bellowing into megaphones, kissing in public, holding hands in front of presidents. Yet there is no evidence that, apart from the impact of AIDS, homosexual promiscuity has abated.[14]

There are several problems with Levin's analysis. First, Levin grossly underestimates the pressures faced by gays today, even in our relatively tolerant American culture. In over two dozen states it is still

---

14. Thomas and Levin, p. 129.

perfectly legal to fire someone simply for being gay. Even where such discrimination is illegal, perceived homosexuality can limit a person's professional and social success in a variety of more subtle ways. Levin should keep in mind that we work in the relatively privileged sphere of academia, where (in some schools, in some ways) homosexuality is indeed largely a "nonissue." But the situation is far different for the vast majority of gays and lesbians in this country. Some work at factories in small Midwestern towns; some live on rural farms; some serve in the military, and so on. We don't all work at Google, alas.

In a similar vein, Levin underestimates the effect of personal history on people's ability to form and maintain successful relationships. While their peers are exploring the exciting, confusing, and terrifying world of dating, gay adolescents often suffer alone in shame and fear. Because adolescents tend to be insecure about their identity and highly sensitive to peer approval, any failure to "fit in" can compound their sense of stigma. Straight teens' habit of making gay jokes is nowhere nearly as deeply ingrained as gay teens' fear of being the object of such jokes: Thus, as the straight teens grow older, they are far more likely than their victims to forget such jokes as "no big deal," while their targets carry the emotional scars for life. A substantial number of gay teens are disowned by their families—the very people whose support most adolescents take for granted. The profound psychological effects of these formative experiences do not disappear simply because Ellen is on TV.

Moreover, Levin's description of the extrinsic explanation is oversimple. True enough, the pressure to remain in the closet is more conducive to furtive encounters than long-term relationships. But there's more to the problem than that. Beyond the already discussed issue of personal history, there's the simple fact that relationships are challenging. Heterosexuals know this, which is why there's a complex web of social structures in place to support them. By and large, gay people don't have such structures—hence the ongoing debate over same-sex marriage.

Indeed, there's an interesting tension in the traditionalist position here. On the one hand, traditionalists claim that "marriage and the family . . . are fragile institutions in need of careful and continuing support."[15] And they point to the increasing prevalence of divorce and premarital sex among heterosexuals as evidence that such support is declining. Yet they refuse to concede that the complete absence of similar support for homosexual relationships might explain many of gays' alleged problems. The critics can't have it both ways: if heterosexual marriages are in trouble despite the numerous social, economic, and legal incentives for keeping them together, we should be little surprised when same-sex relationships—which not only lack such supports, but face considerable hostility—are difficult to maintain.

I'll grant to Levin and Wolfe that for male homosexuality, there's another plausible explanatory factor as well. In general, men of any sexual orientation tend to seek multiple sexual partners more than women do, whether for biological reasons, cultural reasons, or (most likely) both. Thus, populations where men have relationships with men are likely to have higher rates of promiscuity, all else being equal. But to acknowledge this is not to deny that extrinsic and preventable reasons also have a powerful role to play.

I do not mean to absolve gays of personal responsibility for their lives. There is no inconsistency between claiming that people are responsible for meeting certain challenges and claiming that others

---

15. Ramsey Colloquium, p. 19.

are responsible for having needlessly intensified those challenges. Nor do I wish to paint an overly bleak picture of the current situation of gay people in this country. Indeed, one of the most encouraging effects of the debate over same-sex marriage has been to publicize the fact that, despite the aforementioned pressures, there are many gays like me in happy, loving long-term relationships. My point has been to remind critics that they may well share some responsibility for the problems they attribute to homosexuality.

But suppose I'm wrong. Suppose I were to grant—again, purely for the sake of argument—both that the alleged harms exist and that they are caused by homosexuality itself, rather than some external, separable factor. There is still another question that must be asked.

The Third Question: What Follows?

This question is almost universally ignored. The hidden assumption in arguments like these is that if a particular practice is riskier than the alternatives, it follows that the practice is immoral, imprudent, or otherwise to be avoided. But the assumption is pretty obviously false as stated.

Consider some counterexamples: Driving is riskier than walking. Being a coal miner is riskier than being a philosophy professor. Football is riskier than checkers. In each case, the former activity poses a far greater risk of injury (even fatal injury) than the latter. Yet no one believes that driving, coal mining, and football are therefore wrong, or that they should always and everywhere be discouraged by reasonable people. Why not? Because related to the third question is a fourth.

The Fourth Question: Are the Risks in a Given Case Worth It?

Notice that we normally leave this question to competent adults taking the risks. My dental hygienist races cars in her spare time. I think she's nuts for doing so, but I also think it's none of my business. That said, Wolfe is right that society has a stake in its members' behavior and that people should at times vocally oppose others' risk-taking. There's a big leap, however, from that position to the conclusion that we ought to condemn any and all forms of homosexual conduct.

To see why, let's return to the football analogy. Football is responsible for numerous injuries, including serious (occasionally even fatal) head trauma. Now on Wolfe's logic, we ought to ask:

> On the basis of health considerations alone, is it unreasonable to ask if it is better not to be [a football player]? At the very least, don't the facts suggest that it is desirable to prevent the formation of [an interest in football] and to bring people out of it when we can?

After all, there are much safer games, like checkers!

Well, sure. But football players don't want to play checkers; they want to play football. The argument reminds me of an old joke:

QUESTION: What's the best way to avoid spilling your coffee while driving?
ANSWER: Drink tea.

The problem here is not just that the advice is unrealistic or unlikely to be followed. It's that it misses the point. Generally speaking, people choose alternatives they find fulfilling. When those alternatives involve risks, they can take steps to minimize them (like wearing helmets). Some football players, drivers, and coal miners are indeed more reckless than others. So are some sexually active heterosexuals, for that matter. But we don't cite statistics about their problems and conclude that no one should ever engage in any of these activities in any form.

Wolfe responded to my football analogy in a footnote. (See what you miss by not reading footnotes?):

> Corvino's argument that [the risks of homosexual activity] are equivalent to playing football is unpersuasive. Moreover, the idea that a person, by his own activity, might contribute to not just his own early death, but the early death of someone else—especially someone he loves—makes this situation very different from other "high-risk" activities.[16]

Here Wolfe seems not to be paying attention to what I actually wrote. First, I do not argue that the risks of homosexual activity "are equivalent" to those of playing football, though I'm sure that anyone interested in doing a careful analysis would find that many forms of homosexual activity are in fact safer than football. (Wolfe here, like most opponents of homosexuality, seems rather focused on male-male anal sex.) Second, calling an argument "unpersuasive" is no substitute for actually rebutting it. Third, plenty of everyday risky activities put others (including loved ones) at risk, such as driving instead of walking.

Fourth, and most important, Wolfe completely misses the point of the football analogy. The point is not that football is more or less

---

16. Wolfe 2007, p. 106.

risky than gay sex. The point is that "riskier than the alternatives" does not entail "morally wrong." If it did, then no one should ever drive when they could walk, play football when they could play checkers, or have sex of any sort when they could remain celibate.

Most gay people cannot choose to have fulfilling heterosexual relationships. Their choice is not between homosexuality and heterosexuality, but between same-sex relationships and celibacy. Yet within that framework, they also have many other choices: choices about when to have sex, with whom to have sex, how to have sex, and so on. And gays, like everyone else, can make such choices carefully or recklessly.

The only way for Wolfe's argument to work is to assume that homosexual sex in any form is likely to shorten one's lifespan by several decades. In that case, I would agree that celibacy would be the best option for gays. But not even Wolfe believes that assumption. Even if you accepted the ridiculous (or in Wolfe's words, "concededly problematic") Cameron study, and even if you completely ignored the effectiveness of condoms, the most you could conclude is that gay *men* should forgo *anal* sex—which brings me to my next topic.

Anal Sex

In the early 1990s I lived next door to a guy named Jason, who was a born-again Christian rock singer. (Yes, I know this sounds like the premise for a bad sitcom.) While Jason vocally disapproved of my being gay, he was also fascinated by it, and he constantly asked me questions.

One day I revealed to him that I had never had anal sex. His face brightened. "That's awesome!" he shouted.

"Why, pray tell, is it awesome?" I asked.

"Because maybe you'll try it, and then realize you don't like it, and then you won't be gay."

For Jason, being gay meant liking anal sex. He found it strange that the equivalence had never occurred to me. For me, being gay means that I like guys. It means that I have crushes on them, I fall in love with them (one in particular), and I want to "get physical" with them. But it doesn't specify how I should do this.

I suppose the mistake is understandable. Most people would find it bizarre for a heterosexual *not* to desire penile-vaginal intercourse. It's "standard." For some gay men, anal sex is functionally similar—it's what they might call "the real thing." But that's not true for all of us. A guy who's into other guys but prefers oral sex, mutual masturbation, or frottage (look it up) is still gay. Sorry Jason.

Many critics of homosexuality focus on male homosexuality, and particularly anal sex, when discussing the alleged dangers of gay life. This is not surprising. Unprotected anal sex is a particularly apt way of transmitting the HIV virus, a virus that has been responsible for the deaths of legions of gay men and others over the last few decades. These critics needn't embellish the data: I came out in the late 1980s and found AIDS sufficiently frightening. Unlike today, AIDS was then a near-certain death sentence, one that often marked its bearers in visible ways. I am old enough (though just barely) to remember watching acquaintances go from being healthy-looking, to gaunt and lesion-marked, to gone—all in a matter of weeks. While HIV-disease has become far more manageable in the last decade with modern antiretroviral therapies, it is still something I take every precaution to avoid.

Or rather, I *would* take every precaution to avoid HIV if I were in situations that potentially exposed me to it. But as someone who is in a long-term relationship with an HIV-negative partner and doesn't much care for anal sex anyway, HIV is something I seldom think about in a personal way. That's one reason why Wolfe's discussion of fatal diseases, like Tammy's brief rant about anal cancer, seems so remote and inapplicable to me.

To be fair, Wolfe refers to costs "that are often, *though not always*, associated with living as a homosexual," so he recognizes that the connection is not automatic. But the problem remains: Such allegations—even if they were true, or even plausible—provide no reason for me to stop being intimate with Mark, any more than pointing to the town drunk provides me (or any other temperate individual) reason to forgo an occasional glass of wine. It is doubtful that homosexuality is harmful in the ways alleged, and to the extent that it involves risk, it is not clear that those risks are unavoidable, unreasonable, or wrong-making.

Keep in mind that we're not talking about a sport, like football—we're talking about the means for deep human intimacy. So if there's a disanalogy between football and gay sex, it may well be in my favor: I can imagine a life without sports more easily than one without physical intimacy.

Levin's Abnormality

Wolfe's allegations of homosexuality's physical dangers hardly exhaust his case against it. His central argument is a natural law argument—discussed in the next chapter—that escapes the kind of empirical rebuttal I've given thus far. For now, though, I want to turn to a rather different harm argument: one offered by the philosopher Michael Levin, whose comments on promiscuity I discussed above.

Levin and I had a brief correspondence years ago. At the time I was being considered for a point/counterpoint book on gay civil rights; Levin would be my opponent. (Interestingly, the book was ultimately assigned to Levin and Laurence Thomas, who later edited the book that included my exchange with Wolfe.) By way of introduction—and to delay snarky footnotes as long as possible—I sent Levin a copy of my article "Why Shouldn't Tommy and Jim Have Sex?" He wrote back the following surprising note (I didn't save it, so I'm paraphrasing): "Enjoyed reading your 'Tommy and Jim' essay. I see we agree on the morality of homosexuality, though I do consider it abnormal."

Why on earth would someone ask me to write a point/counterpoint book on homosexuality with someone who *agrees* with me on the moral question? I soon learned that Levin was actually a good choice for such a book, partly because he's a smart and engaging writer, and partly because of his interesting (and decidedly nonstandard) position.

Unlike many opponents of same-sex relationships, Levin does not believe that homosexual conduct is immoral. But he does believe that homosexuality is abnormal (a sort of "biological error"), that most gay-rights claims should be rejected, and that it is reasonable for straight people to want to avoid gay people.

Levin expounds his position in the widely reprinted essay "Why Homosexuality Is Abnormal," in a later essay entitled "Homosexuality, Abnormality, and Civil Rights," and in the point/counterpoint book *Sexual Orientation and Human Rights* with Laurence Thomas.[17] In a nutshell, his view is as follows. Gay sex is *abnormal* because it involves using organs in counter-evolutionary ways. Abnormal behaviors tend to cause unhappiness. Since nobody likes unhappy people, it makes sense to avoid gays.

Although Levin's argument invokes proper functions, the unhappiness claim is what drives it. (That's why I address it in this

---

17. Levin 1984 and 1996; Thomas and Levin.

chapter rather than the next one: It is essentially an argument about harm.) If abnormal behaviors did not undermine happiness, there would be no reason to avoid them or people who engage in them. Levin's argument is not simply a version of "The parts don't fit!" Nor is it a statistical observation about how most people use their penises and vaginas: Most people don't put ketchup on their breakfast cereal, but doing so is not "abnormal" in Levin's sense. And Levin's argument doesn't depend on claims about divine intentions (indeed, Levin is skeptical about such claims). So his position is unique in several ways and worth some attention.

What Levin does is to take a commonsense notion and provide it with philosophical grounding. The notion is that penises and vaginas have a function that they are *for*—not in the sense that they were so designed by God, but in the sense that they have some purpose that explains their existence through evolution. Why do people have penises and vaginas, and why do they generally enjoy using them for heterosexual intercourse? Quite simply, it's because their ancestors who did so reproduced successfully, thus passing along genes that coded for similar behavior. From the standpoint of evolution, homosexuality seems surprising—at least at first glance. Assuming an admittedly simplistic evolutionary picture, it would seem that natural selection would eliminate homosexuality over time. Whatever else one might say on the merits of gay sex (and I'm happy to say plenty), it does not seem like a good way to pass along one's genes. Yet homosexuality continues to exist. Why?

One possibility is that genetics play no direct role in causing sexual orientation. Levin, interestingly, rejects that possibility, since he believes, on the basis of recent scientific research, that there is likely a strong genetic element in sexual orientation.[18] Instead, he

---

18. Thomas and Levin, p. 120.

conjectures that homosexuality is a maladaptive trait that exists as a by-product of some adaptive trait, much as sickle-cell anemia appears to be a by-product of malarial resistance. Whatever the precise evolutionary explanation, Levin concludes that "homosexuality is probably as intrinsically maladaptive as it looks." For Levin, gay sex is abnormal because it involves using organs in maladaptive ways.

Levin distinguishes between seemingly abnormal behaviors that still allow normal function and genuinely maladaptive ones; only the latter are abnormal in his technical sense. Humans have ears because the ability to hear helped our ancestors to detect approaching predators (and thus to survive and reproduce), but it is not maladaptive to use them to display earrings or to keep our eyeglasses from slipping off our noses. The difference is that using ears in these ways does not preclude their normal function. Gay sex, by contrast, tends to displace normal heterosexual sex. As Levin writes (discussing the "common sense" version of his position), "This is why homosexuality is abnormal, why male homosexuals are misusing their penises and lesbians their labia: their systematically nonfunctional use of their genitals has usurped their genitals' proper sexual role."[19]

But who cares if gay sex is abnormal in this sense? Here's where Levin connects abnormality with unhappiness. For evolutionary reasons, people tend to find adaptive behaviors enjoyable. Our ancestors who enjoyed adaptive behaviors were more likely to perform them, to survive and to reproduce, and to thus pass along genes that cause their descendants to enjoy performing similar behaviors. For instance, our ancestors who enjoyed using their teeth to chew their food lived longer and produced more offspring, who in turn were genetically "programmed" to enjoy using their teeth in this (normal)

---

19. Thomas and Levin, p. 110.

way. Correspondingly, people tend to find abnormal (maladaptive) behaviors dissatisfying. Levin provides the hypothetical example of Mr. Jones, who removes all his teeth and wears them as a necklace, precluding their normal function. Because of the evolutionary processes that produced him, Jones will likely eventually yearn to chew and feel unhappy at his inability to do so. Those who use their genitals abnormally are likely to feel similar dissatisfaction.

So on Levin's view, evolutionary theory gives us a reason to expect gays to be unhappy. What's more, he suggests that there's independent empirical evidence confirming this expectation. Because no one wants to be around miserable people, it therefore seems rational to avoid gay people—not because homosexuality is evil or immoral, but because it is highly correlated with things ordinary people want to avoid. In Levin's own colorful words:

> Traditionalists are said to find homosexuality "immoral," and no doubt many talk as if they do think this. But I am not sure this is what they have in mind. Traditionalists *deplore* homosexuality, and like most people they utilize the language of disapprobation that is the handiest, namely moral disapprobation, to express themselves. But what they really mean is that homosexuality is disgusting, nauseating, closely connected with fecal matter. One need not show that anal intercourse is immoral to be warranted in wanting to be as far away from it as possible.[20]

Where do I begin?

Let's put aside Levin's typical obsession with anal sex and male homosexuality. Let's ignore, too, the simplistic evolutionary picture

---

20. Thomas and Levin, p. 145.

on which his argument is based. Finally, let us leave alone for the moment Levin's alleged independent evidence for homosexual misery—which suffers from the same defects as Wolfe's—and focus on his unique argument for gay abnormality, which he in turn connects with unhappiness.

The first thing to notice is that Levin's argument is really directed more toward straight people—telling them that it's rational to avoid gays—than toward gay people. Notably, he is not arguing that gay sex is likely to be less satisfying *for gays* than straight sex, though he does think that gay sex is likely to involve a residual dissatisfaction (much like that felt by the gummy Mr. Jones). This is a smart choice on Levin's part, since the idea that gays enjoy gay sex less than straight sex is ludicrous on its face. As Andrew Koppelman puts it, "People tend to want to do what will make them happy, and they don't need Levin to tell them not to pull out their teeth and wear them as necklaces."[21] Gay people engage in gay relationships because they enjoy them, and Levin presumably knows this.

What this means is that Levin's argument provides no reason for me—or people similarly situated—to cease having relationships with same-sex partners. On the contrary, Levin seems bound to recommend the opposite, given his crucial (and plausible) background assumption that it is rational for people to pursue happiness and avoid misery. This makes him something of an anomaly among gay-rights opponents, who generally do hold that homosexuality is not just deplorable or disgusting to outsiders, but intrinsically wrong.

Second, and rather oddly, Levin's argument provides no reason for eschewing bisexuality, provided that penile-vaginal intercourse is a regular part of the bisexual's sex life. In explaining why fellatio,

---

21. Koppelman 1997, p. 83.

masturbation, and other non-coital activities are considered normal for heterosexuals (despite their failure to explain the existence of genitals through evolution), Levin suggests that these are unproblematic as long as they don't supplant coital sex: "Generally speaking, any part of a suite or developmental sequence of behaviors that includes intercourse is normal." Now imagine Bisexual Bob, who regularly has sex with both men and women. Levin's position yields the strange result that Bisexual Bob's "suite" of behaviors—including his homosexual activity—is normal.

Third, notice that Levin's argument is a probabilistic one: if you accept his evolutionary account, you should expect that, in general, straights will be happier than gays. But then what do you do when you meet a happy gay person? Levin claims that homosexuality is a "valid, information-rich proxy" for undesirable traits.[22] This position is increasingly difficult to maintain, as more and more people meet openly gay persons whom they actually like, despite what they otherwise believe about homosexuality. Ask Glenn Stanton, who has spent countless hours on the road with me, considers me a good friend, and has repeatedly said so privately and publicly.

Indeed, it's funny that Levin can lament that "the intelligentsia and the media have been pro-homosexual for three decades" without seeing how this claim upsets a key premise in his argument. Do the intelligentsia and the media like hanging around miserable people? Are they socially blind, or maybe masochists? In any case, the opportunity costs here seem low. If a same-sex couple moves in next door, invite them to your next cookout, and if they turn out to be Debbie Downers, don't invite them back. (Unless, of course, you

---

22. Thomas and Levin, p. 128.

notice them wearing tooth-necklaces, in which case you have my blessing to steer clear of them entirely.)

It is hard to escape the view that, despite his clever evolutionary argument, Levin's real problem with homosexuality is that he finds it—and by extension, gay people—exceedingly yucky. (Recall his claim that "homosexuality is disgusting, nauseating, closely connected with fecal matter"—eeew.) Whether such aversion should be grounds for discrimination in housing, employment, military service, and other sectors—and Levin argues that it should, even apart from his "abnormality" argument—visceral distaste is generally not compelling to those who don't already share it.

But what about those who do share it? I'll grant to Levin that in a free society, people should have wide latitude to avoid others whom they don't like, for whatever reason. If you don't want to invite the couple next door to your next cookout—whether because they're gay, or the "wrong" religion, color, ethnicity, or whatnot—that's your prerogative, even if I would claim that you're exercising it poorly. (Things are different when we're talking about housing, employment, and public accommodations, although discussion of those issues would take us too far afield here.) But is there anything I can say to change your mind?

As a philosopher, probably not. Visceral distaste is generally not susceptible to argument. It is, however, susceptible to exposure, which is one reason why positions like Levin's are so unstable the more visible gays become. If you avoid gays, it's easy to invent a bizarre picture of them or to accept strange images of them as somehow representative. If you actually get to know some, it isn't so easy.

Take Levin's citation of a 1994 essay by a young man dying of AIDS. Levin writes that, because the essay was published in the widely read *New York Times Magazine*, it is "presumably representative of a major strand in homosexual thought":

At this point, let's face it, we're the least innocent of "victims"—we have no excuse, the barrage of safe sex information, the free condoms, blah blah blah.... Well, rubbers break. (Use two or three.) Maybe oral sex without ejaculation isn't as safe as you thought. Maybe the antibodies take more than six months to show up in your bloodstream, so your negative test is no guarantee. The answer? Celibacy, of course. Masturbation, maybe, but be sure to wear rubber gloves. Fantasy. But we, the second wave, we obviously aren't sublimating very well. Maybe the image of death, a dark, sexy man in black, is something we find exciting.... There are days when we don't even remember that it's there, we're so wrapped up in the real tragedy, which is not in our dying, but in our living: applying for ridiculous jobs, filling out forms, selling books to buy food, stealing vitamins. Shoplifting is hard work; so is applying for food stamps, and every pathetic moron of a boss with a part-time temporary position licking out toilet bowls wants a resume, two interviews, work experience and a college degree. It's really getting us down. We are sad so often.[23]

Levin concludes, "It is hard to imagine more loathsome sentiments or a more repellent individual."

Where Levin sees a repellent individual, I see a desperate, angry, dying one. I don't see anything resembling a "major strand in homosexual thought," because such a strand has never existed—and I'm in a far better position to know that than Levin, who proudly avoids gays.

I don't expect Levin to take my word for any of this. But I do expect someone in his position to have a better grasp of the reality of gay and lesbian lives. Levin is a professor at the City University of

---

23. Beachy, p. 127.

New York with a Ph.D. from Columbia, so it's not as if he has to travel to find some of us. Or if he does have to travel, it's only out of his narrow comfort zone.

In recent years, harm arguments against same-sex relationships have fallen largely out of favor—although they surface from time to time among right-wing bloggers, pastors, and pundits, especially whenever some new junk science is released. Instead, we are seeing a resurgence of natural law arguments, which are the focus of our next chapter.

Meanwhile, mainstream Americans have become more attuned to the harms of homophobia. A substantial body of research suggests that lesbian, gay, and bisexual youth are significantly more likely to attempt suicide than their heterosexual peers, and that stigma and discrimination are significant risk factors.[24] Even those who survive such treatment often carry long-term emotional scars. There is something perverse about using moral arguments to inflict harm rather than to alleviate it—and sadly, the harm arguments are more often experienced as weapons than as points of insight.

---

24. Ryan et al.

4 | "IT'S NOT NATURAL"

On Woodward Avenue and 7 Mile Road in Detroit, about a mile from where I live, a massive church is under construction. It's the new headquarters of "Perfecting Church," headed by Pastor Marvin L. Winans, whose smiling face beams from a towering billboard nearby. Whenever I hear the Winans name, I immediately think of the song "Not Natural," recorded by the pastor's younger sisters Angie and Debbie. (Marvin is the fourth of ten siblings; Angie and Debbie are the ninth and tenth.) Written way back when Ellen DeGeneres came out as a lesbian—both on her hit sitcom and in real life—the song begins as follows:

I was chilling on the couch one night
Looking at my screen TV
There were people celebrating and
congratulating the new addition to the Gay Community
I was vexed in the spirit
And began to write this song/It may be cold, but let the truth
   be told
It's not natural
No, that's not the way it goes
It's not natural

Just because it's popular, doesn't mean it's cool
It's not natural
No, that's not the way God planned
It's time for the world to understand

The song provoked an outcry when it was released in 1997. Interviewed in the gay newsmagazine *The Advocate*, Debbie Winans later claimed that "God gave us the lyrics; we simply sang them."[1]

One can't hold Pastor Winans accountable for what his younger sisters say, although he happens to share their view—as do many throughout history. The claim that homosexuality is unnatural has ancient roots. For example, Plato (429–347 B.C.) makes the claim in the *Laws*, despite the fact that his dialogues such as the *Symposium* contain moving paeans to same-sex erotic love. The view endures among gay-rights opponents today, from ivory-tower intellectuals to common cyber-bullies. But what does it mean? It suggests deviance, but not—or not merely—in the sense of statistical abnormality: Ambidexterity is rare, but very few people would call it *unnatural*. The label has normative force, as well as strong emotive connotation: in common parlance, to call something unnatural is to call it grotesque, perverse, monstrous. (Think of zombies.)

That's why the song's lyrics sting: when someone tells you that your romantic longings are not merely sinful but *unnatural*, they might as well tell you that you are less than human. Indeed, some who levy the charge are happy to say just that.

Not everyone who considers homosexuality unnatural singles it out for particular disgust, however. Natural law theorists such as St. Thomas Aquinas (1225–1274) hold that *all* sin is unnatural, because sin is against reason, which is distinctive to human nature.

---

1. Frutkin, p. 22.

Nevertheless, among sexual acts Aquinas reserves the term "unnatural" for those that are deliberately non-procreative (and thus against our animal nature), and he labels these "the gravest kind of sin."[2] His list includes not only homosexuality and bestiality but also masturbation and oral sex—in other words, acts that few people today would think twice about, let alone label unnatural.

The looseness of the term "unnatural" may be part of its rhetorical appeal: it can be tossed around to evoke disgust, without much worry about consistency. Why do many people consider masturbation natural but not homosexual conduct? Why do they consider heterosexual oral sex natural but not homosexual oral sex? Why is it fine for me to use my mouth for licking envelopes, chewing gum, or blowing a horn, but not to use it for romantically kissing a man? And if the answers have something to do with statistical norms ("Well, that's not what most people do") then why don't people consider left-handed writing unnatural, as previous generations did? At times, "unnatural" appears to be nothing more than a rhetorical flourish, invoked to smear things that the speaker finds abhorrent.

If the unnaturalness charge is to carry any moral weight, those who level it should be able to do two things. First, they should be able to specify what exactly they mean, explaining why the label applies to homosexuality but not to other acts that they don't similarly wish to smear.

Second, they should be able to explain why unnaturalness matters morally. Many perfectly innocent actions are unnatural in some sense: wearing eyeglasses, flying planes, cooking food, using iPhones, and so on. Think of that massive Perfecting Church billboard, for example, which is not "naturally" up there in the sky, or the plastic CD containing the Winans album, which does not "naturally"

---

2. Aquinas, *Summa Theologica* II–II, q. 154, a. 12.

produce sound. When people say that homosexuality is unnatural, presumably they mean that we morally ought to avoid it. But why?

Sometimes the implied normative sense of "unnatural" is pretty clear. For example, when someone says, "Don't eat those potato chips, they're loaded with unnatural ingredients," there's an understood connection between unnaturalness and poor health. But that's not the kind of argument I'll be considering in this chapter. If "unnatural" is just a stand-in for "harmful," then we can lump unnaturalness arguments together with the harm arguments considered in the last chapter. But many who levy the unnaturalness charge want to claim that homosexuality is wrong regardless of whether it's harmful: unnaturalness is in this case an independent moral assessment. In what follows, I'll consider some possible meanings of "unnatural," examine whether they apply to homosexual conduct, and evaluate their moral significance.[3]

What Is Unusual or Unconventional Is Unnatural

Let's start with an easy one: unnaturalness in the sense of *statistical abnormality*. It is certainly true that most human beings don't engage in homosexual conduct (unless one considers solitary masturbation homosexual conduct[4]). But so what? Most people

3. This section builds on a similar section from my essay "Why Shouldn't Tommy and Jim Have Sex?" which itself builds on an older essay from Burton Leiser. See Corvino 1997. I'm also indebted to Richard Mohr here and elsewhere for his pioneering work on ethics and homosexuality.

4. I know of no serious thinkers who hold this claim, although some—including Immanuel Kant and the new natural law theorists—hold that homosexual conduct is wrong for the same reason as masturbation (i.e., treating the personal body as a mere instrument of satisfaction). For them, it would be more correct to say that homosexual conduct is a form of masturbation than vice versa.

don't write with their left hands, join monasteries, play the didgeridoo, or put their faces on billboards, either—yet none of these activities are considered wrong simply because they are rare. This sense of "unnatural" misses the term's normative force: to call something "unnatural" is not to *describe* its infrequency but to *prescribe* its avoidance.

This is one reason why it's a mistake for gay-rights activists to place so much emphasis on the oft-cited (and surely exaggerated) claim that gays make up 10% of the population: our numbers are irrelevant when determining whether homosexuality is natural in any morally significant sense. (Pinning down the correct percentage is difficult: Recent studies generally put the number between 2 and 6%, while noting the challenges of identifying stigmatized populations who are frequently not "out" about their identity.[5])

What Is Not Practiced by Other Animals Is Unnatural

I have heard some people—including a number of elected officials—argue, "Even animals know better than to behave homosexually; homosexuality must be wrong." This argument is doubly flawed. First, it rests on a false premise: Homosexual behavior has been documented in hundreds of species, from insects and worms to apes and dolphins, and some animals form long-term same-sex pair-bonds.[6] (There's even a charming children's book based on the true story of

5. See Gates, and Laumann et al.

6. For a review of some studies see Bailey and Zuk. For a more thorough (but older) treatment see Bagemihl.

a male-male penguin couple in the Central Park Zoo who hatched and raised a chick: *And Tango Makes Three*—amazingly, one of the most frequently "banned" books in U.S. libraries.) True, it's unusual for animals to have an *exclusive* homosexual orientation over a long period, although this phenomenon has been observed, interestingly, in domesticated rams.

The argument's second flaw is more important: Even if the premise about animal behavior were true—which it is not—it would not show that homosexuality is immoral. After all, animals don't cook their food, brush their teeth, attend college, or read books; human beings do all these without moral fault. The notion that we ought to look to animals for moral standards is simply facetious, as anyone with house pets will readily attest.

What Does Not Proceed from Innate Desires Is Unnatural

Some people argue that gays are "born that way" and that it is therefore natural and good for them to form homosexual relationships. Others insist that homosexuality is a "lifestyle choice," which is therefore unnatural and wrong. Both sides assume a connection between the origin of homosexual orientation and the moral value of homosexual activity. And insofar as they share that assumption, both sides are wrong.

The idea that all innate desires are good ones is obviously false. Research suggests that some people may be born with a predisposition toward violence, but such people have no more right to strangle their neighbors than anyone else. So even though some people may be born with a homosexual orientation, it doesn't follow that they ought to act on it.

Nor does it follow that they ought *not* to act on it, even if it is not innate. I probably do not have an innate tendency to write with my left hand (since I, like everyone else in my family, have always been right-handed), but it doesn't follow that it would be immoral for me to do so. So even if homosexuality were a "lifestyle choice," it wouldn't follow that it's an immoral lifestyle choice.

The thing to remember is this: There's a difference between something's being natural in the sense of resulting from innate disposition and its being natural in the sense of being morally good. The nature/nurture debate may tell us something about how people come to have the sexual desires they have, but it will not tell us whether it's good for them to satisfy those desires, let alone whether they can—or should—change those desires. I'll devote the entire next chapter to those issues.

What Violates an Organ's Principal Purpose Is Unnatural

Perhaps when people claim that homosexual sex is "unnatural" they mean that it cannot result in procreation. The idea behind the argument is that human organs have various natural or intended purposes: eyes are for seeing, ears are for hearing, genitals are for procreating. According to this position, it is immoral to use an organ in a way that violates its purpose.

This position finds its fullest premodern elaboration in St. Thomas Aquinas, whose teaching forms the basis of much of Roman Catholic moral theology. Aquinas recognizes procreation as sex's purpose and thus labels "unnatural" any intentionally non-procreative sexual acts. He ranks bestiality as the worst of these, morally speaking, followed by homosexual acts, then "not observing the natural manner of copulation" (e.g., heterosexual oral or anal sex), and finally masturbation. He argues that unnatural sexual acts are the "greatest sin among the species of lust": Whereas ordinary sexual sins such as fornication and adultery are merely violations of right reason, unnatural sexual acts violate nature itself.

Aquinas's position has some hard-to-swallow implications. For example, consider an objection that Aquinas himself anticipates:

> It would seem that the unnatural vice is not the greatest sin among the species of lust. For the more a sin is contrary to charity the graver it is. Now adultery, seduction and rape, which are injurious to our neighbor, are seemingly more contrary to the love of our neighbor than unnatural sins, by which no other person is injured.[7]

In response, Aquinas simply bites the bullet and insists that unnatural vices are indeed worse. Whereas rape, fornication, and adultery merely injure human persons, unnatural acts injure God—the Author of nature—himself.

Let us pause to digest this conclusion: According to St. Thomas Aquinas, the authority behind much of Roman Catholic moral teaching, *masturbation is worse than rape.*

One might try to rescue Aquinas here by arguing that a sin's being the worst *among the species of lust* is not the same as its being the worst, period. Unlike masturbation, rape is not just a sin against chastity (i.e., a species of lust) but also a sin against justice. But this move won't work in light of what Aquinas writes here, for according to Aquinas, sins against (human) justice can never outweigh those

---

7. Aquinas, *Summa Theologica* II–II, q. 154, a. 12.

"whereby the very order of nature is violated" and which thus injure God himself.

Alternatively, one might reject Aquinas's stance on masturbation as a function of his mistaken views about human biology, which he largely inherits from Aristotle (384–322 B.C.). Aristotle believed that semen contains the human soul. Aquinas rejects this view (claiming instead that God provides the soul some time after conception) but still believes that the male's "seed" provides the form of the new human being, whereas the female provides only the raw material. The problem with taking this route is that it casts doubt on Aquinas's teachings, not only about masturbation, but also about other "unnatural acts" as well: If "spilling seed" is not next in gravity to homicide, as Aquinas held,[8] then the entire prohibition on non-procreative sexual acts may need to be rethought.

Aquinas's philosophy is more nuanced than his critics (and indeed many of his supporters) sometimes recognize. For example, he rejects the simplistic mapping of human morality onto animal behavior, acknowledges that nature is highly variable, and concedes that humans may permissibly use organs for purposes other than their "natural" ones—it is permissible to walk on one's hands, for instance. Unfortunately, he does not seem to see how such concessions undermine his case against same-sex relations.

In response to the example of walking on one's hands, Aquinas claims that "man's good is not much opposed by such inordinate use";[9] homosexual acts, by contrast, undermine the great good of procreation. There are two problems with this response. The first is that it is by no means clear that procreation is the only legitimate good achieved in sex, or that it is morally necessary for every sexual

---

8. Aquinas, *Summa Contra Gentiles* 3.22.9.

9. Aquinas, *Summa Contra Gentiles* 3.22.9.

act to aim at it. Heterosexual couples often have sex even when they don't want children, don't want more children, or can't have children. Most people recognize that sex has other valuable purposes, including the expression of affection; the pursuit of mutual pleasure; and the building, replenishing, and celebrating of a special kind of intimacy. In order to maintain Aquinas's position, one would have to contend either that those purposes are not genuine goods or that homosexual acts cannot achieve them. These contentions both seem false on their face, although I'll address them at greater length when I discuss the "new" natural law theorists below.

The second problem is that the failure to pursue a good—in this case, procreation—is not equivalent to undermining or attacking that good. Aquinas himself was a celibate monk, after all. As the utilitarian philosopher Jeremy Bentham sharply observed over 200 years ago, if gays should be burned at the stake for the failure to procreate, then "monks ought to be roasted alive by a slow fire."[10] The issue of celibacy aside, there are plenty of heterosexuals who procreate abundantly while also occasionally enjoying, say, mutual masturbation or oral sex to orgasm. Such persons can hardly be said to *undermine* the good of procreation any more than Aquinas himself did.

Incidentally, the argument that gays undermine the good of procreation is sometimes mistakenly attributed to Immanuel Kant (1724–1804 A.D.) in the following form: Homosexuality must be bad for society, because *if everyone were homosexual, there would be no society.* But, first, if everyone were celibate—like both Kant and Aquinas—there would be no society either. Second, the argument doesn't work against people who engage in both homosexual and heterosexual conduct, or who procreate in some other way, such as in vitro fertilization. And third, this argument is not Kantian, since

---

10. Bentham, p. 360–61.

it bases morality on consequences, and Kant is a staunch anti-consequentialist. Kant himself has a rather different argument against homosexual conduct: namely, that it is akin to masturbation, which involves treating the personal body as a mere object. More on this point shortly.

The New Natural Law (NNL) View

The problems with Aquinas's natural law teachings are not news; indeed, they are acknowledged by many of his modern-day admirers. Partly in response to them, an approach has emerged in recent decades known as the New Natural Law (hereafter, NNL) view. The NNL theorists include prominent figures such as Robert George of Princeton, John Finnis of Oxford and Notre Dame, Germain Grisez, Patrick Lee, and various others. Like adherents of the "old" natural law theory, they believe in a set of moral principles that can be known through human reason without appeal to religious revelation. Unlike adherents of the old theory, the NNL theorists hold that "it is not clear . . . that acting against a biological power is necessarily wrong, nor is it clear that sodomitical and other non-marital acts are really contrary to that direction."[11] So they adopt a somewhat different argument against homosexual conduct than Aquinas.

Understanding their argument requires a detour into some dense academic territory. I warn readers now: this is the "thickest" of the chapters, philosophically speaking. Hang in there! The detour is necessary because the NNL theorists offer the most intellectually

---

11. George 1999, p. 181.

sophisticated moral argument against same-sex relations currently available. Although their view is sometimes difficult to grasp, it captures widely held intuitions about the unique moral character of male-female unions.

Perhaps the best way to approach NNL theory is to begin by contrasting it with a more familiar moral theory: utilitarianism. According to utilitarians, an act is right insofar as it promotes the best consequences—often understood in terms of the "greatest happiness for the greatest number"—it is wrong insofar as it produces bad or harmful consequences. Utilitarians thus think of morality in terms of social welfare: In evaluating same-sex relations, they would ask "Do such relations make people happy?" and "Do they hurt anyone?" and then weigh the pros and cons. (Although I am putting this all rather simplistically, utilitarian theory can be as sophisticated as any other.) In light of the last chapter, it is not surprising that utilitarians generally have a positive view of same-sex relations: Bentham, the theory's progenitor, is a good early example, having written an unpublished defense of homosexuality in 1785.

NNL theorists reject this approach. For them, morality is not primarily about making people happy (or minimizing their pain), especially if happiness is understood in terms of subjective pleasure. It is about conforming our behavior to our given nature as human beings. Although the NNL theorists believe that God designs our nature, they also believe that we can know (most of) morality's demands without appealing to religious revelation. To do so, we must grasp certain basic goods, which are intrinsically compelling reasons for action. These goods include life and health, knowledge and aesthetic experience, friendship, integrity, and various others. Such goods are "basic" in the sense that they cannot be reduced to one another or derived from more general goods: Instead, they must be known through direct insight and defended dialectically. To put it another way, you either "get" that these things are good, or you don't.

Some have criticized the NNL view for asserting premises without evidence. But in fairness, the "you either get it or you don't" point is true for the basic premises of any moral theory. Take utilitarianism. If asked, "Why is it good to educate children?" a utilitarian might answer, "Because it promotes general happiness." But if then asked, "Why is happiness good?" a utilitarian would be hard-pressed to provide a further argument, in the sense of an inference from premises to a conclusion. If you don't "get" the value of happiness, the best someone can do is to try to jog your intuitions by drawing out the implications of accepting or rejecting the view. And that's precisely what the NNL theorists do for their basic goods.

Among the basic goods that the NNL theorists recognize is *marriage*, understood in a special, personal, nonpolitical sense: the comprehensive, "two-in-one-flesh" union of a male and female. While marriage in this sense may result in happiness, emotional and physical health, and so on, its purpose is not reducible to any of these. Nor is it reducible to procreation—which is a common misreading of the NNL view. For the NNL theorists, sex may never be properly chosen merely as a means to some other thing, children included. It is to be chosen for the sake of marriage, the comprehensive union, itself.

As a *comprehensive* personal union, marriage includes both mental and physical dimensions, which reinforce each other. On the mental level, it requires a loving, permanent, exclusive commitment between the partners. On the physical level, it requires that the partners unite biologically in conjugal acts. Such acts make them "literally, not metaphorically, one organism."[12] So there's something truly

---

12. George 1999, p. 183 n. 23.

special about penis-in-vagina sex (coitus) that puts it in an entirely different moral class from other sexual acts. It unites the male and female as a single organic reproductive whole: in common language, the "two become one."

Problems with the NNL View

The most common objection to NNL theory concerns heterosexual couples known to be permanently infertile: the "sterile-couples" objection. Imagine a woman whose cancerous uterus has been removed. Her sex with her husband cannot result in procreation, and they both know it. It would therefore seem that their sexual acts are no more capable of creating a genuinely reproductive union than the same-sex couple's, and that consistency requires that we treat both cases the same: If the sterile heterosexual couple is morally permitted to have sex (as everyone grants), then so is the same-sex couple.

In my public talks, pro-NNL audience members have occasionally suggested that the sterile heterosexual couple could still get pregnant by way of a miracle. But if a woman without a uterus can get pregnant by way of a miracle, then so can a pair of lesbians, and so, for that matter, can I. Besides, suspending the physical laws of nature is not going to help *natural* law theorists, and sensibly enough they do not take that route.

Instead, they answer that although the sterile heterosexual couple cannot reproduce, their sexual acts—unlike the same-sex couple's—can still be "of the reproductive type." Because their coitus is still coordinated toward the common good of reproduction, it can still unite them as a single organism, even if reproduction is neither intended nor possible. NNL theorists Sherif Girgis, Robert George, and Ryan Anderson attempt to explain with an analogy:

When Einstein and Bohr discussed a physics problem, they co-ordinated intellectually for an intellectual good, truth. And the intellectual union they enjoyed was real, whether or not its ultimate target (in this case, a theoretical solution) was reached—assuming, as we safely can, that both Einstein and Bohr were honestly seeking truth and not merely pretending while engaging in deception or other acts which would make their apparent intellectual union only an illusion.

By extension, bodily union involves mutual coordination toward a bodily good—which is realized only through coitus. And this union occurs even when conception, the bodily good toward which sexual intercourse as a biological function is oriented, does not occur.[13]

The problem with this explanation is that there's a big difference between a goal which "does not" occur even though people are "honestly seeking" it, and a goal which *cannot* occur, and which thus cannot be honestly sought by anyone aware of its impossibility. NNL theorists regularly blur this difference.

The heterosexual couple who know themselves to be permanently infertile cannot seek conception in their sexual acts. They are akin to a pair of scientists who mull over a problem which they know to be insolvable. There may be value in such mulling—a flexing of the mental muscles, perhaps—but that value has nothing to do with a solution, because the solution is known to be impossible. Similarly, there may be value in the sterile heterosexual couple's coitus, but that value has nothing to do with reproduction, because

---

13. Girgis, George, and Anderson, p. 254.

reproduction is known to be impossible. Calling their coitus an act of the "reproductive type" is misleading.

It can be misleading in other cases as well. "Reproductive type" acts are not necessary for reproduction, because procreation can be achieved by in vitro fertilization without coitus. And they are not sufficient for reproduction, because of the many cases where uncontracepted coitus does not result in procreation. What sense, then, can we make of the term "reproductive type"? As far as I can discern, it essentially refers to nothing more or less than *coital* sex: penis in vagina. (Or perhaps, coital sex without contraceptives: NNL theorists differ on this point[14]).

If that's what "reproductive type" indicates, then it indeed follows that sterile heterosexual couples can engage in reproductive-type acts whereas same-sex couples cannot. But several questions remain: Is being of the reproductive type—that is, achieving organic bodily union in coitus—really what's morally important about sex? Moreover, is it the only moral good sex can achieve, or might there be others, including ones that don't require coitus? And even if non-coital sex could not achieve any genuine moral goods, as the NNL theorists claim, why must it be positively *bad*—as opposed to, say, just a harmless pleasurable activity? Let us take these questions in turn.

First, on the special moral value of coitus: As I see it, what makes coitus uniquely morally important is its propensity to create new life. That's a grave moral responsibility if anything is. Moreover, I grant that there's something awe-inspiring about the fact that we are literally flesh of our parents' flesh, created via their union and connected to them and our grandparents and so on in an unbroken

---

14. The NNL theorists (of whom I'm aware) who have commented publicly on this question deny that contracepted sex can be of the reproductive type. See for example George 2006, p. 160 n. 59.

biological chain. I respect the NNL attempt to give special moral weight to procreation.

Unfortunately, the attempt fails. Rather than giving special moral weight to procreation, the NNL theorists give special moral weight to "reproductive-type" acts which are neither necessary nor sufficient for procreation. By their own admission, the value of such acts has no more to do with actual procreation than the value of jointly mulling over a known-insolvable physics problem has to do with finding a solution: The point is the bodily union, not its potential results.

NNL theorists claim that such unity gives spouses a reason to engage in coitus even if they cannot procreate and even if they don't particularly enjoy coitus. I, by contrast, think that unless you and your partner are trying to procreate, you should go for whatever safe, healthy and consensual sexual acts you find mutually fulfilling. If that's coital sex, great. If that's oral sex, great. If you want to dress up in furry costumes and chase each other around the bed? Knock yourselves out.

Recall that basic goods are fundamental reasons for action—they are intrinsically action-guiding. It is worth observing that marriage—as a two-in-one-flesh organic bodily union—was not included on lists of basic goods until relatively late: Finnis mentions it in 1996, but not in 1980; Grisez includes it in 1993 but not in 1983.[15] Perhaps most telling is the fact that natural law theorists who are not particularly concerned with condemning homosexual conduct don't include it at all.[16] It is hard to escape the impression that, far from

---

15. See Finnis 1980, pp. 86–90, Finnis 1996, p. 5, Grisez 1983, pp. 121–22, Grisez 1993, p. 568.

16. See Murphy, p. 96, Chappell, p. 43, Gomez-Lobo, pp. 10–23.

identifying a genuine good, the NNL account of "marriage" is just an artificial construct designed expressly for including sterile heterosexual couples while excluding same-sex couples.

This problem relates to the second question: whether bodily union—and ultimately, marriage, in the NNL sense—is the *only* good achievable by sex. Consider the goods people usually associate with sex. "Organic bodily union" is generally not on the list. Procreation sometimes is, but neither the sterile heterosexual couple nor the homosexual couple can achieve procreation. There are others, however: the expression of a certain kind of affection, the building of intimacy, and shared pleasure, to name a few. The NNL theorists must either deny that these are genuine goods or else deny that non-coital sex can achieve them. Such denials fly in the face of common sense.

The general claim underlying these denials—and the answer to our third question, *Why is non-coital sex positively bad?*—is that for NNL, non-coital sexual acts are tantamount to mutual masturbation, and masturbation is always wrong. Such acts are wrong for two related reasons. First, they involve the *illusion* of bodily union instead of genuine union, and it is always wrong to pursue a counterfeit good instead of a real good. Second, and related, they treat the personal body as a mere instrument for producing an effect (sexual pleasure) in consciousness. According to Robert George and Patrick Lee, in such a choice "one regards the body as outside the subject, and so as a mere object. A certain contempt for the body inheres in such choices."[17] (Notice the Kantian theme about treating the person as a mere instrument.)

In my view, this account just badly mis-describes what partners seek, and genuinely experience, in sex—including non-coital sex. To use a fancy philosopher's term, it's bad sexual phenomenology.

---

17. George 1999, p. 164.

Consider a man who enjoys performing cunnilingus with his wife to express affection and experience mutual pleasure. He need not be choosing such an activity as a counterfeit version of coitus. He might choose it, rather, in order to please his wife, a result that in turn pleases him. Such an act constitutes a genuine expression of affection, and it may facilitate each partner's emotional and physical well-being. It may be a special intimacy that they reserve only for each other, something that enhances the bond between them. There is no reason to think that, in performing it, the couple "regards the body as outside the subject," whatever that means. They are bodily persons expressing affection in a bodily way, and that real bodily experience, which they know to be intensely pleasurable, is what they choose. They would not be satisfied, we may presume, with an "experience machine" that would give them the subjective sensation of sex, or that would simply fill their brains with endorphins. They seek genuine personal interaction in the form of non-coital sex.

The NNL theorists insist that in non-coital sex, "the physical activities (stroking, rubbing) are chosen merely as extrinsic means of producing an effect (gratification) in consciousness, *the only thing chosen for its own sake.*"[18] But they give absolutely no evidence for this strange claim, and it is not the sort of thing one can know from one's armchair.

This point raises another question, about how to determine exactly which acts NNL prohibits. The example just cited relates to female orgasm, about which natural law theorists say very little. Instead, following Aquinas—and nearly every other philosopher who writes on these matters—they tend to focus on male orgasms and semen. (As legal philosopher Andrew Koppelman notes, "The possibility of female orgasm appears to be an embarrassment to the

---

18. Lee and George 1999, p.155 (emphasis added).

theory."[19]) NNL permits fellatio and other non-coital activities only as foreplay on the way to reproductive-type acts. But what about various arousing activities that may, but need not, lead to male orgasm: kissing, stroking, licking, erotic massage, and so on? What about cuddling? In ordinary romantic life—for gays as well as straights—the line between the sexual and the nonsexual is typically not so sharp. There is no obvious point where one starts choosing gratification for its own sake, and it's hard to imagine that NNL would condemn *all* these activities unless they were followed by coitus. It would be interesting to see the NNL reasons—if there are any—for why gay *kissing* might be unnatural.

I conclude that the NNL theorists have mis-located the moral value of sex, and that even if there's something distinctively valuable about coitus (apart from its procreative potential), they have failed to show what it is, let alone that other forms of sex are positively bad. The very same things that make non-coital sex valuable for heterosexual partners—expression of affection, experience of mutual pleasure, physical and emotional well-being, and so on—make it valuable for same-sex couples as well.

Unnaturalness: Concluding Thoughts

It is worth adding that any view that rests the wrongness of homosexual conduct on the wrongness of masturbation ought to face a severe burden of persuasion. The fact that many people approvingly cite natural law theory to condemn homosexuality while ignoring its other conclusions says a great deal about people's capacity to tolerate inconsistency in the service of prejudice. Like Aquinas, the

---

19. Koppelman 2002, p. 86.

NNL theorists label masturbation, contraception, and non-coital heterosexual sex unnatural for the very same reasons that they label homosexual sex unnatural: the failure to achieve a reproductive-type union. They even condemn non-coital sex for heterosexuals unable to achieve coitus (say, because of injury). I suppose one can give them credit for consistency even while blanching at their coldness.

For the rest of us, it often seems that an act is unnatural when the person making the claim finds it abhorrent or revolting. Thus homosexuality, but not masturbation; eating dog meat, but not eating pork; interracial relations generally, but not John Rolfe and Pocahontas. (Prior to being struck down in 1967, Virginia anti-miscegenation law defined anyone with "one-sixteenth or less of the blood of the American Indian" as white, in order "to recognize as an integral and honored part of the white race the descendants of John Rolfe and Pocahontas."[20]) "Unnatural" according to this view is simply a term of abuse, a fancy word for "disgusting," a way to mask visceral reactions as well-considered moral judgments. We can do better.

---

20. See *Loving v. Virginia,* footnote 4.

5 | "BORN THIS WAY"

The headline read, "'Homosexuality Is a Choice,' Says Homo-Journo: Yeah, Our Jaw Dropped Too."[1]

I was the "Homo-Journo" in question, although I'm not sure when I earned that title, and I have yet to add it to my resume. The headline appeared on Queerty.com, a pro-gay website, regarding a column I wrote, and the ensuing brief story provoked a litany of "How dare he!" comments. Clearly this "Homo-Journo" had some explaining to do.

It all started when New Mexico Governor Bill Richardson, then a presidential candidate, appeared at a forum sponsored by the Human Rights Campaign, a gay-rights group, which aired on LOGO, a gay cable network. At one point, rock-singer Melissa Etheridge, one of three panelists asking questions, jumped in with a softball: "Do you think homosexuality is a choice, or is it biological?"

Richardson, who has a strong gay-rights record, responded, "It's a choice. It's . . ."

Several audience members gasped. Etheridge quickly interrupted, "I don't think you understand the question," prompting nervous laughter throughout the studio. She tried again: "Do you think

---

1. The piece appeared on the website Queerty.com in the summer of 2007, though it is no longer accessible there.

I—a homosexual—is born that way, or do you think that around seventh grade we go, 'Ooh, I want to be gay?'"

"Seventh grade" is right: At that moment Etheridge sounded like an indulgent schoolteacher, trying to feed a quiz answer to a hapless student. Multiple-choice: A or B (Hint: Obviously not B). But Richardson missed the hint. Instead of saying, "Well, it's certainly not a choice in *that* sense," he started rambling on about not being a scientist or some such.

Audience reaction, and the subsequent commentary, all suggested that his performance was a disaster. One editorial referred to it as his "macaca moment" (recalling Virginia Senator George Allen's politically fatal use of that racial slur during his 2006 campaign). How could Richardson not realize that when a gay person asks, "Is it a choice?" it's like when your wife or your mother asks, "Does this dress make me look fat?" The answer is always, unequivocally, *No.*

Or at least that's the official answer. The real answer is more complex—and it depends on what question is being asked. That's why I wrote the column that provoked the Queerty headline: I personally think Etheridge's question, and much of the debate over this issue, is confused.

Yes and No

Take Etheridge's first formulation: "Do you think homosexuality is a choice, or is it biological?" The question actually jumbles together two distinct issues:

1. How do people become gay? (By genetics? Hormones? Early environment? Some combination of the above?)
   and
2. Can they change it (i.e., choose to be otherwise)?

A fancy way of saying this is that the question conflates an *etiological* issue (what's the cause or origin of sexual orientation?) with a *phenomenological* one (how do you experience your sexual orientation?). These two issues vary independently. My hair color is genetically determined, but I can change it. The fact that I understand English is environmentally determined, but I can't change it. (Of course I could learn a new language, but it would never subsume my native one at this point.) Some "choices" can be undone, some cannot; some biologically "hardwired" attributes can be "re-wired," some cannot. That an attribute feels deep and fixed tells us little about how it got there.

Of course, Melissa Etheridge does have a point: no one just wakes up one day and says, "Ooh, I want to be gay." Given anti-gay discrimination, hardly anyone would want to. Even the lesbian feminists who claim that their sexual orientation is chosen don't claim that it happens by arbitrary whim. So that part of Etheridge's question should have been easy—even for someone with little exposure to homosexuality. After all, no one wakes up and says, "Ooh, I want to be straight" either.

So we must be born this way, right?

Wrong. Put aside the fact that "this way" is ambiguous. (No one is born having sex—that, obviously, involves choices). The crucial point is that the leap from "I don't choose my feelings" to "I was born this way" is a nonsequitur. It forces a decision between (A) voluntarily chosen and (B) genetically hardwired, without entertaining possibilities like (C) acquired but nonvoluntary. Etheridge's formulation makes the false dilemma stark: The only alternative she offers to "born this way" is "Ooh, I want to be gay."

"Born this way" is a virtual article of faith among gays—so much so that the singer Lady Gaga's song of the same title has been touted as a gay anthem. Call me a heretic, but I neither know nor care whether I was born this way. I don't remember the way the world was when I was born, and I can't discern my genetic makeup by simple introspection. All I know is that I've had these feelings for a long time, they're a deep fact about me, and they're not something that I can readily change, even if I wanted to. (I'll say a little bit about so-called reparative therapy later on.) These facts are all compatible with a variety of competing scientific explanations of sexual orientation, including environmental ones.

There's also something odd about asking whether a trait is "biological." We're flesh-and-blood creatures, so at some level, *everything* about us is biological. Even my decision to wear a blue shirt today—a "choice" if anything is—has some biological substrate involving synapses in the brain and whatnot. So the real question is not "Is it biological?" but "What's the biological story here?" Is my attraction to men genetically hardwired, such that it was predestined upon conception? Was it influenced by chemical experiences in the womb? Am I biologically predisposed to have certain personality traits, which, when placed in the right sort of environment (or "wrong" sort of environment, depending on your view), might or might not lead to such attraction? What effect, if any, do formative social experiences have on my current desires?

These are all interesting scientific questions. They are not the sort of questions on which politicians, or rock singers, or "homo-journos" have any special expertise. In that respect, Richardson's profession of scientific ignorance was both modest and reasonable. (Note: Because I'm interested in a moral question and not an etiological one—and because scientific knowledge in this area continues to develop— I will not review the scientific literature here. Interested readers are encouraged to do further research.[2])

---

2. A somewhat dated but still excellent book on that research, its limitations and its relevance, is Edward Stein's *The Mismeasure of Desire.*

What about the other question: Is it a choice? Again, it depends. If we mean, "Do people choose their same-sex attractions?" the answer is *no*: we discover our feelings; we do not invent them. I said as much in the original column.[3] If we mean, "Do people choose their same-sex relationships?" my answer is "I hope so." No one is shackling me to the bed with Mark (and if someone were, that would be none of your business). In this sense, homosexuality involves choices just as heterosexuality does. They're not choices about what kind of feelings to have, but about whether, when, and how to act on those feelings. When Richardson said "it's a choice," perhaps he meant that we should have the right to make such choices. If so, good for him.

Similarly, when gay-rights opponents say "it's a choice," they might mean that the so-called homosexual lifestyle is a choice. In one sense, they're absolutely right. As ambiguous as the phrase "homosexual lifestyle" is, it surely refers to choices. While I didn't choose my attraction to men, I choose to be an "out" gay man. I choose to be with Mark (and am proud of that choice). I choose to speak and write openly in defense of gays and lesbians. And so on. I could have chosen otherwise, which doesn't mean that I *should* have chosen otherwise.

The subtext—one might say "baggage"—behind "it's a choice" is that homosexuality involves a kind of defiance: heterosexuality is the "normal" or "default" setting, and it's only by some act of willful deviance that people become gay. This latter claim is not only patently false, it's offensive. It ignores the deep struggle many of us go through as we become aware of our same-sex attractions. It ignores

---

3. Corvino, "Richardson was Right—Sort of " igfculturewatch.com June 23, 2012 at http://igfculturewatch.com/2007/08/20/richardson-was-right-sort-of/.

the fact that, far from embracing homosexuality, many spend years fighting or hiding it. Perhaps that's why this issue hits such a raw nerve. Do opponents think I'm doing this just to be difficult? To upset my parents? To offend church elders? They could not be more wrong.

When I Knew

Every coming-out story is unique, though there are common themes. Mine is fairly typical—at least typical for a male growing up in the 70s and 80s in an Italian-Catholic family in suburban New York. Let me digress from philosophizing for a while to engage in some illustrative autobiography.

It's always hard to pinpoint when one became aware of one's homosexuality, because much of that awareness is prearticulate, and only after the fact can one label it correctly. Yes, that "special friendship" in high school was a romantic crush, but what about that guy I always noticed in junior high? And what about my obsession with Rocco, the older brother of Christine, my best friend in third grade? Only in hindsight do I recognize such longings as manifestations of homosexuality.

Usually, when gay people refer to their "coming out," they mean when they started telling other people. But coming out isn't a single event: it's a process—one that begins well before you utter the words and continues indefinitely. Every time a stranger on an airplane asks me, "Are you married?" I have to decide whether to come out.

I attended Chaminade High School, an all-male Catholic prep school on Long Island. By the time I arrived there, I knew that I had "gay feelings," but I denied that I was gay. It was a beautiful example of the human capacity for keeping separate sets of mental books: I knew I had "gay feelings," I knew I didn't have "straight feelings" (though I never dwelled on this fact), and I knew—as any rational person would—that a person with gay feelings but no straight feelings is gay. But I claimed I was "basically straight." (This, from someone who would later teach elementary logic.) Somehow, by not allowing ideas to "touch," I could refuse to draw the obvious conclusions from them.

I admitted my "gay feelings" (it's an odd phrase, invented only to stave off the reality *I'm gay*) to very few people. I told priest-confessors, who were generally sympathetic: "It's okay as long as you don't act on them; relax," they often said. I also told a psychologist. In tenth grade I developed a crush on a close friend, and it deeply troubled me. I asked my parents to send me to a therapist without explaining why I wanted to go; humanely, they did so without prying. Like the priests, Dr. Buxter told me to relax; unlike them, she offered no negative judgment about the behavior. This shocked me. I was a devout Catholic, and I believed that these feelings manifested, as the Church taught, "an objective disorder towards an intrinsic moral evil." I wanted them to go away. I prayed—a lot—to be healed.

Aside from the priests and Dr. Buxter, I shared my struggles with no one. I certainly didn't seek sexual contact with other males—that would have been unthinkable. Nor, incidentally, did I masturbate: I was *very* Catholic, and more than a bit naïve. My "evil" activities were, by virtually any reasonable standard, innocuous. I remember the tremendous guilt I would feel when the new calendars hit the store shelves each fall, and I would surreptitiously pick up the ones with the shirtless men, gazing on their beauty with longing and shame. (Today, I have a habit of picking up such calendars with a deliberate swipe, just to prove that I can, even though I now find them cheesy and unappealing.)

By the time I reached college—St. John's University in New York—I had mustered the courage to admit my "gay feelings" to only one close friend. Martin had been my best buddy since junior high. As it turns out, he too was gay, although he didn't tell me that until many months after I came out to him: Somehow (maybe through "gaydar") I could sense that he was a kindred spirit. Martin was the person I rushed to the morning after my prom night, my first and only attempt at "making out" with a girl. It felt weird—and frightening, since it confirmed something I wanted to avoid—and I needed to "process." So as soon as the limo dropped me home, I hopped in my '74 Monte Carlo and drove to his house. It was 6 a.m., and I stood in his backyard in a rented tux, throwing clothespins at his window to rouse him without waking his parents. When his mother finally entered the kitchen, she glanced at me and asked, "Oh, John, would you like an English muffin?"—as if there were nothing unusual about early-morning guests in black tie.

I'm not sure if it was during that conversation or a later one when I finally told Martin, "Yes I have these feelings, but if I'm gay I'm not ready to admit it." It was true: I still couldn't wrap my mind around *I'm gay*. I was ramming against the closet door, yet I could only barely crack it open.

I continued to confide in priests. I had contemplated entering the priesthood myself throughout my time at Chaminade, and by the time I entered college, I was a candidate with the Capuchin Franciscan order. This development was crucial for two reasons: First, the Capuchins were the first people to directly challenge me on my sexuality. As an official candidate, I attended "discernment weekends" to discuss, among other things, the prospect of lifelong celibacy. "There's a difference between being celibate and being asexual," we were told; "priests are still physical beings." The Capuchins knew there were gays among us, and we openly discussed the issue. "We don't care whether you're gay or straight," my vocation director explained to me one day, "but we do care about your being self-aware."

Second, for the first time in my life I met other openly gay people. During one of our discernment weekends, I attended a lecture by Fr. Richard, a gentle man to whom I had taken an immediate liking. At one point he uttered the words, "As a gay man . . ."

. . . and I ran screaming from the room.

Okay, not really. But I was floored by the admission. My shock was only compounded when later that day, my friend and fellow candidate Scott told me, "Me, too." The light started to shine through my cracked closet door, and I desperately tried to avert my eyes. "Not me! Not me! I just have 'gay feelings'!!! I'm not like the rest of you!"

Fr. Richard's lecture was a gateway to my real "Road to Damascus" moment, which came a few months later. I was at an end-of-the-semester party at the home of one of my theology professors, and I was chatting with my classmate Tony. Though I only knew Tony casually, I was always attracted to him. He had a ready smile and a goofy charm that stood in sharp relief to my uptight demeanor. He also had the lithe physique of the young Kevin Bacon, one of my onscreen "crushes," though I wouldn't have called it that then.

The party was on the south shore of Long Island, not far from where my parents kept a boat. I started telling Tony about the boat, and I suggested that it would be fun to hang out there sometime. I didn't directly invite him to go there that evening, but I strongly hinted at the possibility. Thankfully, he didn't take the bait. I say "thankfully" because Tony is straight: That, combined with my messy state of mind, would have made for a rather awkward night. Tony and I left the party separately.

But as I drove home I could not stop thinking about him. To be precise, I could not stop thinking about me thinking about him. My inner voice started addressing me in the second person: "You like

Tony, don't you? You wanted to go home with Tony, didn't you? You wanted to go home with Tony! You've got a crush on Tony! You don't just have gay feelings, John. *You're gay.*"

My inner voice. It wasn't scolding, but it was firm. At the time, given my religious worldview, I identified it with God or the Holy Spirit; today, as a nonbeliever, I might call it conscience or just my reflective self. But it was addressing me forcefully, and I couldn't ignore it. *You've got a crush on Tony. You're gay.* For me, the coming-out "moment" didn't involve me telling someone else. It was me telling me. From that night forward, there was no more "basically straight but with gay feelings." I could still say it, but I knew I'd be lying.

Within days I told Martin, Scott, and my vocation director (all of whom essentially responded with a "duh!"). Within a week I told my parents and my good friend Darlene, who later dated Tony. (That was a source of much mirth between us: "Well, Dar, since I can't have him . . .") And yes, I eventually told Tony, who was a complete sweetheart about it. If my profession of interest made him uncomfortable, he never told me.

I say that my coming-out story is somewhat typical. Here's one respect in which it probably isn't. Many gay men come out—start telling people—well after their first sexual or romantic contact with other males. For me, it was the other way around. It would be months before I first kissed another guy, a year before I got naked with one, and nearly eighteen months before I had sex with one—if those awkward early fumblings count as sex. Yet I was openly gay among friends and schoolmates throughout this time. For me, it was a matter of honesty. As a devout Christian, I believed in witnessing to the truth. The truth about me was that I was gay—not "straight with gay feelings," but gay. And I strongly believed at the time that God was speaking this truth to me. "Enough hiding—this is who you are—be true to yourself."

I don't know that I would have said "God made me this way." "Made" is past tense, and at the time I believed that God was continually making me—not to mention everything else in existence, in all its complexity. In my philosophy and theology classes I struggled with the question of how, if a benevolent, omnipotent God creates everything, there is evil in the world. (Quick, unsatisfying answer: evil is the absence of God—*but isn't God everywhere?*) I did not take the fact that my gayness felt deep and permanent as proof that it was okay to be gay. Not all deep facts about us are good. I just knew that I was gay, and I believed that God wanted me to know this. I had no idea what he wanted me to do with it, which is one reason I kept coming out to friends, priests, professors—anyone from whom I could seek advice.

Can I Change It?

And so I didn't choose to be gay, at least not in any direct or conscious way. I don't rule out the possibility that choices I made early in life might have indirectly influenced my sexual orientation, though I very much doubt that if (for example) I had played more football, I wouldn't be attracted to guys. No: If choices affect sexual orientation, the effect is likely subtle: perhaps my avoidance of sports, combined with affinity for food, which led to my being slightly chubby during adolescence, helps explain my preference for slim guys. But don't ask me; ask scientists. I can tell you what; I can't tell you why.

Notice, too, how difficult it is to tease factors apart. My "choice" to avoid sports or to eat extra dessert stemmed from preferences which themselves might have been strongly genetically influenced. Remember, we're flesh-and-blood creatures: *all* our desires, preferences, and choices have some biological substrate.

Some gay-rights advocates reject the term "sexual preference" in favor of "sexual orientation" on the grounds that "preference" smacks of arbitrariness: I prefer to go to the movies rather than stay home, but I might change my mind. They're right that sexual orientation can't be turned on and off at whim, but they're wrong if they think that preferences are voluntary. I prefer black coffee to coffee with cream and sugar. I can force myself to drink sweetened coffee, but that doesn't mean that I'll like it or would choose it given alternatives. Preferences can be more or less fixed: a person who prefers country life to the hustle and bustle of the city might retain such preferences no matter how many times she visits Manhattan. So whether we call it "sexual preference" or "sexual orientation," our romantic attraction patterns are not the sort of thing over which we have direct voluntary control. As W. H. Auden writes in his poem "Canzone," "When shall we learn, what should be clear as day, We cannot choose what we are free to love?"

Let me say just a few words here on "Reparative Therapy" or "Sexual Orientation Change Efforts" (SOCE), to use the American Psychological Association's preferred terminology. (I refer the reader to the APA's *Report of the Task Force on Appropriate Therapeutic Responses to Sexual Orientation*, available online, for a more detailed treatment.[4]) First, a conciliatory note: I believe we should give others the same respect that we ourselves demand, and that includes giving people wide latitude about living their lives as they see fit. If you really believe that you're heterosexual deep down, and you want

---

4. APA Task Force on Appropriate Therapeutic Responses to Sexual Orientation. *Report of the Task Force on Appropriate Therapeutic Responses to Sexual Orientation*. Washington, DC: American Psychological Association, 2009, accessed June 27, 2012 at http://www.apa.org/pi/lgbt/resources/therapeutic-response.pdf.

to take steps to help realize that identity, far be it from me to demand otherwise. I'll let you be the expert on what you feel deep down, as long as you show me the same courtesy.

In fact, many self-identified "ex-gays" do not show me the same courtesy. I've had several tell me, "C'mon: Deep down you know that being gay is wrong." I know no such thing, and I resent it when other people tell me what I know "deep down." So let's make a deal: You don't tell me what I know deep down, and I won't tell you what you know deep down.

Much of the time, however, SOCE is not sought voluntarily by people who desire it deep down: It's imposed by parents, often on frightened, vulnerable teenagers who can be deeply damaged by it. The risk of damage is not just my opinion; it's the overwhelming view of mainstream health professionals. As the APA report explains, "The American Psychological Association Task Force on Appropriate Therapeutic Responses to Sexual Orientation conducted a systematic review of the peer-reviewed journal literature on sexual orientation change efforts (SOCE) and concluded that efforts to change sexual orientation are unlikely to be successful and involve some risk of harm, contrary to the claims of SOCE practitioners and advocates."[5]

And that's my biggest concern about these "Reparative Therapy" efforts: They frequently do more harm than good, often to vulnerable youth who experience lasting psychological scars as a result. A recent Worth Health Organization report called such efforts "a serious threat to the health and well-being—even the lives—of affected people."[6]

---

5. APA Task Force on Appropriate Therapeutic Responses to Sexual Orientation, p. v.

6. "'Therapies' to Change Sexual Orientation Lack Medical Justification and Threaten Health." paho.org, June 27, 2012 at http://new.paho.org/hq/index.php?option=com_content&task=view&id=6803&Itemid=1926.

I have some related concerns as well. First, there's the tendency to promote myths about the so-called homosexual lifestyle by generalizing from some people's unfortunate personal experiences. Ex-gay spokespersons will often recount, in lurid detail, a life of promiscuity, sexual abuse, drug addiction, loneliness, depression, and so on. "That is what I left behind," they tearfully announce, and who can blame them? But that experience is not my experience, and it's not typical of the gay experience. To suggest otherwise is to spread lies about the reality of gay and lesbian people's lives. (The best antidote for this is for the rest of us to tell our own stories openly and proudly.)

A second concern is the abuse and misrepresentation of science. Many SOCE practitioners are engaged in "therapy" even though they are neither trained nor licensed to do so; as noted, some of that "therapy" can cause lasting psychological damage. Ex-gay ministries often lean on discredited etiological theories: domineering mothers, absent fathers, and that sort of thing. They also tend to give false hope to those who seek such therapy. Even the staunchest adherents of SOCE admit that only a tiny fraction of those who seek change achieve any lasting success, and even then it's unclear whether feelings, or merely behaviors, have been changed. It's worth noting that Dr. Robert Spitzer, the noted author of a 2003 study endorsing the use of such therapies, recently recanted the study and issued an apology.[7]

The third and related problem is that some ex-gay programs promote not merely a "change" but a "cure." (The major programs, like Exodus, a religious organization, and NARTH, an ostensibly secular one, tend to eschew such language.) "Cure" implies a disease or

---

7. See Carey.

medical disorder, which homosexuality is not. "Spiritual" disorders are another matter, but then we've left the realm of science for that of religion. And ex-gay ministries have an unfortunate habit of conflating science, religion, and politics.

So when ex-gays announce, from billboards and magazine ads, that "Change is possible," I say: Possible? Maybe. Likely? No. Desirable? Not for me, thanks—and probably not for most, given the documented risks.

The Essentialist/Constructionist Debate

There is an academic field known as "queer theory" that criticizes traditional categories of gender and sexuality (among others) and instead argues for the social and historical character of identity. Recently, some gay-rights opponents have appealed to the work of queer theorists to offer a kind of "gotcha!" argument: since these theorists admit that homosexuality is socially constructed, it follows that homosexuality is neither deep nor fixed. Aha!

This argument is mistaken at least twice over, and proves that a little theory can be a dangerous thing. First, the queer theorists hold that *all* sexuality is constructed, not just homosexuality. So if their view implies that homosexuality is neither deep nor fixed, it would imply the same thing about heterosexuality. Whoops.

But, second, the queer theorists' view implies no such thing. Even if sexuality is socially constructed, it doesn't follow that it's superficial. Here's David Halperin, a prominent social constructionist: "Just because my sexuality is an artifact of cultural processes doesn't mean I'm not stuck with it. Particular cultures are contingent, but the personal identities and forms of erotic life that take shape within the horizons of those cultures are not. . . . I don't mean that I can't inquire into, criticize, or try to understand how I came to be what I am, but no amount of conscious reflection will enable me simply to walk away from my socialization and acquire a new cultural (or sexual) identity."[8]

So the opponents' argument starts with a bad misreading of queer theory (artificially narrowing it to homosexuality) and then draws an invalid inference from it (assuming that "constructed" implies "voluntary"). Perhaps books on queer theory should come with a disclaimer: "For professional use only. Please do not try this at home."

One might object that I'm being too quick here (and admittedly, queer theory is not the sort of thing that lends itself to a breezy treatment). Surely, "socially constructed" implies "voluntary" in some sense?

To answer that question, I need to broach the essentialist/constructionist debate. I'm going to wade into deep and volatile waters, but there is so much misunderstanding about this debate, especially in popular circles, that it deserves some attention.

Essentialists hold that sexual orientation is an objective, intrinsic, and culturally independent property of persons. Thus essentialists would claim that there were gays in ancient Greece, for example, even though the Greeks would not have thought of themselves in quite those terms. Constructionists, by contrast, hold that sexual orientation is cultural and historical: Prior to the late 19th century, when the term "homosexual" was coined, there was no such thing as a gay person in the usual sense. Of course, the constructionists do not deny that there were same-sex desires or same-sex sexual acts before that time. Rather, they claim that those desires and acts did

---

8. Halperin, p. 53.

not constitute a "sexual orientation"—because that mode of identity simply didn't exist until fairly recently. (Note that, for the same reasons, the constructionists would claim that there were no *straight* people prior to the 19th century either.) To use an analogy, although prior to the 16th century there were Christians who objected to the Roman Catholic Church's teachings, there were no "Protestants"—that identity occurs only in a particular historical context.

Many people suspect that essentialists and constructionists are arguing past each other: Essentialists seem more interested in sexual desire, whereas constructionists seem more interested in sexual identity. There is, however, a vital point of agreement between the camps: They agree that in virtually every time and culture, there have been people who desire sexual intimacy with persons of the same sex. We can worry later about whether such persons "count" as gay or understood themselves as such. But either way, they exist, and both essentialists and constructionists agree that they exist. They also agree—and this is crucial—that these persons' desires are usually not "voluntary" in any meaningful sense.

Regarding the question of whether "socially constructed" means "voluntary": the answer is, yes and no. Culture results from choices, and in that sense it's voluntary. But it certainly doesn't follow that by some individual act of will I can divorce myself from my cultural context. And even if I could, altering my context doesn't eradicate my desires—it simply changes how I frame and express them.

Before moving on from the essentialist/constructionist debate, it's worth asking how it lines up with the nature/nurture debate. Despite what everyone seems to think, it doesn't line up well at all.

Take first the essentialists. Essentialists hold that sexual orientation is a "real," cultural independent property of persons. They needn't subscribe to any particular theory about how it gets there: genetics, environment, or some combination of the two. So essentialists need not choose "nature" over "nurture" to remain consistent essentialists.

What about constructionists? Constructionists must reject the claim that there is a gene for sexual orientation: That would be precisely the sort of culturally independent property that essentialists embrace and constructionists deny. But the claim that genes "make us gay" is simplistic—especially on a constructionist worldview. Genes influence desires indirectly, by coding for the development of certain physical structures. They do not capture the richness of our social and historical identity. So there's no reason why a constructionist can't accept biological explanations for sexual desires while maintaining that such explanations are only part of the picture of who we are. And there's even less reason to think that a constructionist must reject such explanations in favor of classic environmental ones: domineering mothers and such. Constructionists can accept a wide variety of scientific accounts—including ones emphasizing genetic factors—without abandoning their conviction that science only tells us part of the story (and probably not the most interesting part).

Social constructionist theory may seem arcane, but here's one way it might be useful: It highlights the simplistic ways in which people think about sexual orientation, especially in the context of the nature/nurture debate. For instance, we have genes that influence the development of our lungs, larynx, mouth, and the speech areas of our brain. Yet no one thinks we have a gene for "speaking," much less one for "speaking English." When it comes to sexual orientation, however—a complex human trait if ever there were one—people jump right into discussions of "the gay gene."

Who Cares If We're "Born This Way"?

Having established that sexual orientation is not a matter of voluntary choice—and that, even if it were, it would not follow that being gay is a bad choice—why does it matter if we're "born this way"? I think it's because people mistakenly take "born this way" to imply a number of other claims:

1. *If I'm born this way, then homosexuality is an "immutable characteristic."* As argued above, this conclusion doesn't follow. Whether you're born with a trait and whether you can change it are separate issues. I was born with brown hair, but I can dye my hair blond, inadvisable as that may be. Conversely, that a trait is acquired doesn't mean that it's changeable. Again, my comprehension of English is acquired, but short of a lobotomy I can't change it (though I could certainly add other languages).

2. *If I'm born this way, then I can't be blamed for it.* Certainly, no one should be blamed for traits they're born with (putting aside the theological notion of original sin). Even the Roman Catholic Church acknowledges that "the particular inclination of the homosexual person is not a sin." But that still leaves open whether one would be blameworthy for acting on the inclination.

3. *If I'm born this way, then I have a right to be this way.* Again, we need to distinguish between inclinations and actions. Even though you have a right to whatever feelings you have, your right to act on them depends on their content. Alcoholism may have a genetic basis, but it doesn't follow that anyone has the right to drink excessively. Congenitally blind people may feel like driving, but they don't have the right to do it. Whether you have

a right to do something is independent of the origin of the disposition towards it.

Fortunately, being "born this way" is not necessary for making a rights claim. Religion is an acquired trait, yet most Americans support religious freedom. The Supreme Court even recognizes religious affiliation as a "suspect classification," worthy of heightened scrutiny against discrimination.

4. *If I'm born this way, then it's not a disorder.* That conclusion doesn't follow either. Many disorders have a genetic basis. This is not to say that homosexuality is disordered. Whether a trait is disordered depends on its effect on individuals and society, not on where it comes from.

   This last point is important in light of some of the sillier environmental explanations for homosexuality. Let's suppose it were true, despite ample evidence to the contrary, that homo-sexuality is caused by a domineering mother and absent father. Even then it would not follow that homosexuality is disordered. Consider a counterexample: If domineering mothers caused their children to be more kind, would kindness become a disorder? Of course not.

5. *If I'm born this way, then it's "natural."* As I argued in the last chapter, "natural" is a slippery term. Being born gay wouldn't prove that gayness is any more "natural" than any other congenital trait, positive or negative. This is not a helpful sense of "natural."

6. *If I'm born this way (and only if I'm born this way), then it's a deep and important fact about me.* Sorry, but no. Some people are born with vestigial third nipples, but that's hardly a deep fact about them. On the other hand, people aren't born with their religious commitments, yet many consider them deep and important. A trait's depth and importance are independent of whether one is born with it.

I am not denying that sexual orientation is deep, important, and for most people relatively fixed. All those things are true. Nor am I denying that genetic explanations for homosexuality have a powerful *psychological* role to play in promoting acceptance. For better or worse, people who believe gays are "born that way" are statistically more likely to support gay rights. Genetic explanations are also useful in convincing parents that their child's homosexuality is not their "fault" ("If only I had played more football with Junior!"). But a bad argument for a nice conclusion—even a *true* conclusion—is still a bad argument. I for one don't want my rights to hinge on either poor logic or ongoing scientific controversy.

Conclusion: A Word about the Race Analogy

Before moving on to the next chapter, I want to say a bit about the analogy between sexual orientation and race, which often lurks in the background of the "Born This Way?" debate. As I noted, one doesn't have to be born with a trait for it to be deep, important, and worthy of civil rights protection. (Religion is a good example.) But gay-rights opponents sometimes object to any analogy with the civil rights movement on the grounds that "race and sexual orientation are not the same thing!"

Of course race and sexual orientation are not the same thing. An analogy doesn't mean that two things are the same; it means that they're similar in some relevant respects. They may be quite dissimilar in other respects, and often both the similarities and the differences can be instructive.

According to gay-rights opponents, one key difference is that race is an "immutable, non-behavioral characteristic," whereas homosexuality involves chosen behaviors; thus it's wrong (even insulting) to compare the two. But even apart from the evidence for a genetic contribution to sexual orientation, this objection is badly misguided. It misunderstands the nature of racism, the nature of homophobia, and the point of the analogy between the two.

Although race is in some sense "an immutable, non-behavioral characteristic," racism is all about chosen behaviors. The racist doesn't simply object to people's skin color: he objects to their moving into "our" neighborhoods, marrying "our" daughters, attacking "our" values, and so on. In other words, he objects to behaviors, both real and imagined. What's more, discriminating on the basis of race—dividing up the world according to skin color and treating people differently because of it—is most certainly a chosen behavior. Calling race "non-behavioral" misses that important fact.

At the same time, calling homosexuality "behavioral" misses quite a bit as well. Yes, homosexuality (like heterosexuality) is expressed in behaviors; some sexual, some not. But one need not be romantically active to be kicked out of the house, fired from a job, or abused verbally or physically for being gay. Merely being perceived as "queer" (without any homosexual "behavior") is enough to trigger discrimination. Even where chosen behaviors trigger it, it doesn't follow that they *warrant* it. And that's the main point of the analogy: Both traits subject the bearer to discrimination, often in the name of "nature" or "God's law," without good justification.

I grant that there are important differences between race and sexual orientation, as well as between racism and homophobia. It is hard to usefully compare *anything* to slavery (which is not to deny some horrible abuse visited on LGBT people throughout history and today). Moreover, gays and lesbians do not face the cumulative generational effects of discrimination in the same way that ethnic minorities do: Typically, our parents, grandparents, and so on were all heterosexual. On the other hand, no one is kicked out of the house because their biological parents figure out that they're black. The absence of generational continuity means that sexual minorities often lack the family support and empathy that ethnic minorities take for granted—indeed, sometimes their families are the worst source of abuse.

In any case, while there is little to be gained from claims of "my oppression is more significant than yours," there is much to be gained from studying the lessons of history. What it teaches us in both cases is that otherwise decent people sometimes visit harsh treatment on those they perceive to be "different."

Of course, just because some moral taboos (like the ban on interracial relationships) are cruel and unjustified, it doesn't follow that all are. And that brings us to the topic of our next chapter.

6 | "MAN ON MAN, MAN ON DOG, OR WHATEVER THE CASE MAY BE"

Back in 2003, when Rick Santorum was the U.S. Senate's third-ranking Republican, an Associated Press reporter asked his opinion on laws prohibiting homosexual conduct. (At the time, the U.S. Supreme Court was preparing to rule in *Lawrence v. Texas*, ultimately striking down such laws in a 6-3 majority.) The senator responded:

> I have a problem with homosexual acts.... [I]f the Supreme Court says that you have the right to consensual sex within your home, then you have the right to bigamy, you have the right to polygamy, you have the right to incest, you have the right to adultery. You have the right to anything. Does that undermine the fabric of our society? I would argue yes, it does....

> Every society in the history of man has upheld the institution of marriage as a bond between a man and a woman.... In every society, the definition of marriage has not ever to my knowledge included homosexuality. That's not to pick on homosexuality. It's not, you know, man on child, man on dog, or whatever the case may be.[1]

---

1. "Excerpts of Santorum's AP Interview," 2003.

Reaction to Santorum's now-infamous "man on dog" remarks was swift and sharp. Sex-advice columnist Dan Savage even launched a successful internet campaign to associate Santorum's name with a nasty byproduct of anal intercourse. Santorum, for his part, has never apologized for the remarks, although in recent years he has denied that he was comparing homosexuality with bestiality and child sexual abuse. During his 2012 Republican presidential campaign he told CNN's John King: "I said it's *not* those things. I didn't connect them. I specifically excluded them."[2] This denial sounds unconvincing. When Santorum said that it's *not* man on child, man on dog, and so on, the *not* was there to distinguish traditional heterosexual marriage from a list of bad things. In his view, homosexuality clearly belongs on the bad list.

That doesn't mean, of course, that Santorum sees these things as equally bad. Analogies compare things that are similar in some respects, which is not the same as saying that they're identical in all respects. If you're in a particularly charitable mood and willing to overlook some parts of the interview, you can read Santorum's remarks as making a claim about the logic of privacy rights: if people have the right to do *whatever* they want in the privacy of their own homes, then they have the right to bigamy, polygamy, incest, adultery, bestiality, and so on. Or at least, they have the prima facie or presumptive right, which could be overridden only by some stronger countervailing right, such as other people's right not to be harmed. (That countervailing right would quickly rule out "man on child" sex, not to mention many instances of other things on the list.)

Having said that, it's difficult to maintain a charitable mood when someone mentions your consensual adult relationships in the

---

2. http://transcripts.cnn.com/TRANSCRIPTS/1201/04/jkusa.01.html (emphasis added).

same breath as "man on child" and "man on dog" sex. Whatever anyone says about Santorum's remarks as a matter of logic—and I'll have plenty to say in this chapter—they were thoughtless and nasty as a political sound bite. Even some of his fellow Republicans thought he had gone too far.

It's not just Rick Santorum who invokes the slippery slope. U.S. Supreme Court Justice Antonin Scalia made a similar argument in his scathing dissent in *Lawrence v. Texas*, as did Justice Byron White in *Bowers v. Hardwick,* which *Lawrence* reversed.[3] So have William Bennett, Hadley Arkes, Charles Krauthammer, and a host of other prominent conservative writers. In the colorful words of John Finnis, those who defend gay sex "have no principled moral case to offer against . . . the getting of orgasmic sexual pleasure in whatever friendly touch or welcoming orifice (human or otherwise) one may opportunely find it."[4]

In the past I've referred to this slippery-slope argument as the "PIB" argument, short for "polygamy, incest, and bestiality," although other items sometimes make the list as well.[5] What got me interested in PIB, aside from my wanting to defend gay people against nasty smears, is that it isn't entirely clear what the argument is saying. Is it predicting that once homosexuality becomes more accepted (some of) these other things will become more accepted as well? Is it making a logical point, suggesting that even if the things won't ensue,

3. Justice Byron White used the analogy in the 1986 U.S. Supreme Court Decision *Bowers v.* Hardwick (478 U.S. 186 [1986]), and Justice Scalia used it in his dissent in the 2003 *Lawrence v. Texas* (539 U.S. 02-102 [2003]). See also Charles Krauthammer, "When John and Jim Say 'I Do,'" *Time*, July 22, 1996; William Bennett, "Leave Marriage Alone," *Newsweek*, June 3, 1996; Hadley Arkes, "The Role of Nature," from the hearing of the House Judiciary Committee, May 15, 1996; all three are reprinted in Sullivan.

4. Finnis 1997, p. 34.

5. Corvino 2005.

in fact, they're somehow related in principle? Or is it primarily a rhetorical move, simply trying to scare people away from homosexuality by invoking a parade of horribles? In many ways, the PIB argument seems more like a question or a challenge than an argument proper: "Okay, Mr. or Ms. Sexual Liberal, explain to me why all these other things are wrong." Most people aren't prepared to do that on short notice, which makes the PIB point a debater's dream: It's a handy sound-bite argument that doesn't lend itself to a handy sound-bite response.

One way to approach the PIB argument is to turn the challenge around and ask, *What does one thing have to do with the other?* Polygamy can be heterosexual or homosexual, and the societies that practice it tend to be the least accepting of same-sex relationships. Incest can be heterosexual or homosexual. Bestiality, I suppose, can be heterosexual or homosexual, although like most folks I prefer not to think about it too carefully. Since there is no inherent reason to classify PIB with homosexuality rather than heterosexuality, we must ask, What's the connection?

There are two main answers to this question, and they give us the two broad versions of the PIB argument: a *logical* version and a *causal* version. (Note: calling one version the *logical* version does not mean that it is particularly reasonable or that the other version is *illogical*: it just means that the argument is based on logical connections rather than empirical ones.) Let's take each in turn.

PIB Argument: The Logical Version

The logical version of the PIB argument, which is the one that philosophers usually favor, says that the argument for same-sex relationships makes an equally good case for PIB relationships. In effect, it claims that the pro-gay argument "proves too much": if you accept it, you commit yourself to other, less palatable conclusions. So the logical PIB argument is what philosophers call a *reductio ad absurdum* ("reduction to absurdity"), a way of showing that certain premises—in this case, those establishing that same-sex relationships are morally permissible—have absurd implications. It doesn't matter whether approval of homosexuality actually leads to approval of these other things. The point is not to make a prediction: It's to indicate the alleged logical inconsistency of supporting homosexuality while opposing PIB.

But why would anyone think that supporting same-sex relationships logically entails supporting PIB? The answer, I think, is that some people misread the pro-gay position as resting on some version of the following premise: *People have a right to whatever kind of sexual activity they find fulfilling.* If that were true, then it would indeed follow that people have a right to polygamy, incest, "man on child, man on dog, or whatever the case may be." But no serious person actually believes this premise, at least not in unqualified form. That is, no serious person thinks that the right to sexual expression is absolute. The premise, thus construed, is a straw man.

A more reasonable premise suggests that sexual expression is an important feature of human life which must be morally balanced against other features of human life. For most people, sex is a key source of intimacy. It is a conduit of joy and sorrow, pride and shame, power and vulnerability, connection and isolation. Its absence—and especially its enforced denial—can be painful. On the other hand, there are good moral reasons for prohibiting some sexual relationships, either individually (say, because Jack's relationship with Jane breaks his vow to Jill) or as a class (say, because the relationship is unfaithful, or emotionally unhealthy, or physically harmful, or morally defective in some other way). So for any sexual relationship—and for that matter, any human action—we must ask: Are there good reasons for it? Are there good reasons against it? There is no reason to think that the answers to those questions will be the same for homosexuality as they are for polygamy, incest, or bestiality—which are as different from each other as each is from homosexuality. Each must be evaluated on its own evidence.

We have spent the last five chapters examining the moral evidence surrounding homosexuality. The basic case in favor of it is straight-forward: For some people, same-sex relationships are an important source of genuine human goods, including emotional and physical intimacy, mutual pleasure, and so on. That positive case must be balanced against any negatives—although, as we have seen, the standard objections fall apart under scrutiny.

What about PIB? I don't doubt that *some* PIB relationships can realize genuine human goods. Polygamy is the most plausible candidate: It is quite common historically, and there may well have been circumstances (for example, a shortage of men due to war or other dangers) that made it work well in particular societies. But that's only half the story. The other half requires asking whether, despite these goods, there are overriding reasons for discouraging or con-demning polygamy today. Polygamous societies are almost always *polygynous*, where one husband has multiple wives. (Polyandry—one wife with multiple husbands—is by contrast quite rare.) The usual result is a sexist and classist society where high-status males acquire multiple wives while low-status males become virtually unmarriageable. Thus, from a social-policy point of view, there are reasons to be wary of polygamy. Perhaps those reasons could be overcome by further argument, but the central point remains: Argu-ments about the morally appropriate *number* of sexual partners are logically distinct from arguments about the morally appropriate *gender* of sexual partners.

The same is true for incest arguments: whether people should have sex with close relatives (of either sex) is a distinct question from whether they should have sex with non-relatives of the same sex. Some might wonder whether the problem with incest is that it poses genetic risks for offspring, an objection that wouldn't apply to gay incest. But the reason for the incest taboo is not merely that off-spring might have birth defects (a problem which can be anticipated via genetic testing, and which doesn't apply past childbearing age). It is also that sex has a powerful effect on the dynamics of family life. As Jonathan Rauch vividly puts it:

> Imagine being a fourteen-year-old girl and suspecting that your sixteen-year-old brother or thirty-four-year-old father had ideas about courting you in a few years. Imagine being the sixteen-year-old boy and developing what you think is a crush on your younger sister and being able to fantasize and talk about marrying her someday. Imagine being the parent and telling your son he can marry his sister someday, but right now he needs to keep his hands off her.... I cannot fathom all of the effects which the prospect of child-parent or sibling-sibling marriage might have on the dynamics of family life, but I can't imagine the effects would be good, and I can't imagine why anyone would want to try the experiment and see.[6]

These problems apply just as much to homosexual incest as to heterosexual incest.

There is another important disanalogy between the incest ban and the homosexuality ban. The incest ban means that every person is forbidden to have sex with *some* people—a relatively small

6. Rauch, p. 132.

group—whom he might find romantically appealing: his close relatives. By contrast, the homosexuality ban means that gay people are forbidden to have sex with *anyone* whom they might find romantically appealing. Unlike the incest ban, it reduces their pool of available romantic partners to zero—an infinitely greater restriction.[7] One could make a similar point about the polygamy ban: in principle, any man who can fall in love with two women can fall in love with one, and any woman who can fall in love with an already-married man can fall in love with an unmarried one.

What about bestiality—Santorum's "man on dog" example? It's hard to know what to say here, except that I share most people's revulsion to it. Of course there's the issue of consent. On the other hand, we do plenty to animals without their consent, including many uncontroversial interactions. While bestiality is often harmful to animals, it need not be: there's an urban legend that comes to mind involving a woman, a dog, peanut butter, and a surprise party. (Feel free to Google it.) Ultimately, the problem with bestiality seems to be less about the effect on the animal than the effect on the person, damaging his or her capacity for appropriate human relationships.

I made this latter point in an article entitled "Homosexuality and the PIB Argument," which prompted a reply from Christopher Wolfe.[8] Wolfe agrees with me that bestiality is likely to damage a person's capacity for human relationships. But he worries that I appear to "back off" the argument and speculates that I must be afraid to say that any consensual act not harmful to others is immoral.[9] As you are probably aware by now, I have no such fear. To

---

7. Rauch, p. 127.

8. Corvino 2005, Wolfe 2007.

9. Wolfe 2007, p. 101.

the extent that I back off the personal-damage argument, it's because I haven't done the relevant research and don't really care to. For all I know, zoophiles are some of the most psychologically healthy people in the world, have great sex with their (human) spouses, and so on. And if that were so, Wolfe and I would have to find some other argument in order to maintain our objection, or else conclude that bestiality's wrongness is a fundamental moral fact.

Wolfe then contends that if I say that bestiality is intrinsically immoral, I open up a space for him to argue, analogously, that homosexuality is intrinsically immoral. This is wishful thinking at best, utter confusion at worst. The whole point of claiming that some action-type is *intrinsically* immoral is to say that its immorality does not depend on the wrongness of other action-types; its wrongness does not derive from some more general principle. It is entirely possible—and I would add, quite common—for someone consistently to believe that sex with animals (of any sex) is intrinsically immoral but that sex with persons of the same sex is not. Gay-rights advocates are as entitled to basic premises as anyone else. But basic premises about bestiality do not entail basic premises about homosexuality—or any about other behavior.

I'm reminded here of a funny story from Dan Savage. Savage was on a radio show with a man who sincerely claimed to have a romantic (including sexual) relationship with a horse. At the end of the interview, as the wrap-up music was playing, Savage offhandedly said, "Oh, I forgot to ask—is it a male horse or a female horse?" The man turned red, glared at Savage, and retorted indignantly, "I AM NOT GAY!!!" (I suppose people find comfort where they can.)

One might try arguing that since PIB and homosexuality have traditionally been grouped together as wrong, the burden of proof is on anyone who wants to take an item off the list. But this response fails twice over. First, the "tradition" that groups these things together is actually a relatively modern artifact: Polygamy, as noted, was a very common form of marriage historically, and it is accepted (indeed, encouraged) in various cultures today.[10] Homosexuality has been condemned in many cultures, but certainly not all.[11] Indeed, same-sex eroticism has been celebrated in the art and literature of great civilizations.[12]

The second problem with this response is that just because practices *have been* grouped together as wrong, it doesn't follow that they *should be.* This is especially obvious when we consider other things that were once common taboos, such as interracial sex. And while strict assignments of burden of proof may work in courtrooms, in everyday life the burden of proof (or at least, the burden of persuasion) is on whoever wants to prove something. Both sides are in the same boat there.

One might argue that homosexuality, like bestiality, is always non-procreative. That's true, but it doesn't explain why polygamy (which is abundantly procreative) and incest (which can be procreative, though often with disastrous results) land on the same list. Moreover, as we saw in chapter 4, there is no good reason to think that all sex must be open to procreation. The more one examines the PIB argument, the more it appears that opponents just lump together things they don't like and then dare others to challenge the list. Of course, until one knows why the list members were initially grouped together, it's impossible to offer a reason why some item doesn't belong or to argue that the removal of one doesn't require the removal of others.

---

10. For an excellent history of marriage, including polygamy, see Coontz.

11. For a comprehensive discussion of homosexuality (and attitudes toward it) in history, see Crompton.

12. Again, see Crompton.

What if the PIB-plus-homosexuality list is simply a collection of morally wrong sexual practices, each one there for its own reasons? In that case, the logical form of the PIB argument would collapse: Its whole point is that PIB and homosexuality are logically related. If the various items are immoral, but for unrelated reasons, the following analogy would apply: it would be like putting various useful objects on my desk for different reasons—a pen for writing, a lamp for reading, a letter-opener, a stapler, a paperweight, and so on—and then arguing that if I remove the lamp I have to remove the stapler and the paperweight. Besides, as we have seen in previous chapters, the arguments for judging homosexual conduct immoral simply *don't work*. There was no good reason for putting homosexuality on the list in the first place.

I conclude that the best response to the logical version of the PIB argument remains the simple one we started with: *What does one thing have to do with the other?*

PIB Argument: The Causal Version

The foregoing discussion assumes that the PIB argument alleges some logical connection between PIB and homosexuality. There's another possibility, however. Perhaps the connection is not logical but empirical. That is, perhaps the endorsement of one item *will* lead to the endorsement of others, whether or not it logically should. For instance, maybe the wider acceptance of homosexuality will embolden polygamists and make it harder for others to resist their advocacy.

This is the causal version of the PIB argument. It typically ignores incest and bestiality—and from here on, so shall we. Because it focuses instead on polygamy, it usually refers to same-sex *marriage* rather than homosexual acts. (There is no such thing as a "polygamous act," strictly

speaking, although one might refer to a pattern of behavior as polygamous *conduct*.) So our discussion will now focus more on public
policy, and specifically marriage, than on the morality of relationships
per se.

The best-known proponent of the causal PIB argument is Stanley
Kurtz, who claims that the slippery slope to polygamy is "[a]mong
the likeliest effects of gay marriage."[13] Kurtz has been predicting
this pro-polygamy effect since the mid-1990s. But his evidence for
it is thin, and his evidence for polygamy's connection with homosexuality is even thinner. He writes:

> It's getting tougher to laugh off the "slippery slope" argument—
> the claim that gay marriage will lead to polygamy, polyamory,
> and ultimately to the replacement of marriage itself by an infi-
> nitely flexible partnership system. We've now got a movement
> for legalized polyamory and the abolition of marriage in Sweden.
> The Netherlands has given legal, political, and public approval
> to a cohabitation contract for a polyamorous bisexual triad. Two
> out of four reports on polygamy commissioned by the Canadian
> government recommended decriminalization and regulation of
> the practice. And now comes *Big Love*, HBO's domestic drama
> about an American polygamous family.[14]

This paragraph nicely encapsulates the kinds of exaggerations and
outright falsehoods that typify discussion of this issue.

First, in 2006, when Kurtz wrote the above paragraph, Sweden
didn't have "gay marriage": it had "registered partnerships," the kind
of "separate-but-equal" status most same-sex-marriage advocates
typically oppose—as should anyone worried about an "infinitely

---

13. Kurtz 2003.
14. Kurtz 2006.

flexible partnership system." Second, Kurtz's case of the "polyamorous bisexual triad" was not a marriage at all, but a private cohabitation contract signed by a Dutch notary public. The relationship was neither registered with nor sanctioned by the state: it was no more a legal polygamous marriage than a three-person lease agreement is a legal polygamous marriage. Third, the fact that some Canadian studies of polygamy recommended decriminalization and regulation is hardly evidence of widespread support for the practice. And fourth, the success of the HBO series *Big Love* signaled a wave of support for polygamy about as much as the success of *The Sopranos* signaled a wave of support for the Mafia.

Kurtz's deeper problem is that he fails to show any causal connection between these alleged phenomena and gay rights. He has tried to establish one by looking at marriage trends in Scandinavia, but his analysis falters on the fact that these trends substantially predated same-sex marriage there. (William Eskridge and Darren Spedale's *Gay Marriage for Better or for Worse?: What We've Learned from the Evidence* provides a book-length refutation.)

Kurtz has also tried to establish the connection by arguing that some of the same people who endorse polygamy also endorse same-sex marriage, and that they invoke the same "civil rights" language in both cases. This is true but entirely inconclusive. Some of the same people who oppose abortion also oppose capital punishment and invoke the same "sanctity of life" language, but that's no reason to conclude that one movement leads to the other. In fact, the vast majority of the world's polygamy supporters are religious fundamentalists who strenuously *oppose* homosexuality, and the practice tends to appear in U.S. states (like Utah, Nevada, and Texas) with the *lowest* support for gay rights. Indeed, to the extent that the gay-rights movement promotes an egalitarian view of the sexes, it will likely undermine common forms of polygamy. Kurtz can link the two movements only by selective myopia.

Kurtz has also tried to connect the two issues via the issue of infidelity. He notes that polygamous societies tend to have high rates of infidelity, because they promote the idea that men "need" multiple women. Such infidelity is problematic because it causes instability for wives and for children, many of whom are born outside of marriage. How does Kurtz then connect this problem with homosexuality? His logic seems to go like this: Polygamous societies have high rates of infidelity; gay males have high rates of infidelity; therefore, the gay-rights movement will lead to polygamy—presumably by weakening the norms of fidelity that hitherto kept polygamy at bay. *If we let gays marry*, Kurtz seems to be saying, *then straight men will start cheating on their wives.* Even if this prediction were plausible—which it isn't—the conclusion hardly seems justified.

First, on the prediction's implausibility: Kurtz is basing his argument on the premise that gay male couples tend to be less sexually exclusive than either heterosexual couples or lesbian couples. Even Kurtz admits, "Lesbians, for their part, do value monogamy."[15] His worry seems to be that if we allow same-sex couples to marry, gay males' sexual infidelity will bleed into the general population. But he never explains how. Keep in mind that gay men and lesbians make up a relatively small minority of the general population.[16] Gay men make up about half of that minority, *coupled* gay men an even smaller subset, and *coupled gay males in open relationships* a smaller subset still. In Jonathan Rauch's words, "We might as well regard nudists as the trendsetters for fashion."[17]

---

15. Kurtz 2003.

16. No one knows exactly how many, due to the problems of self-reporting among a stigmatized population. Most reasonable estimates are between 2 and 6%. See Laumann et al., ch. 8.

17. Rauch, p. 153.

While sexual exclusivity may be challenging, it's not so challenging that a sexually exclusive couple (straight or gay) can't look at a sexually open couple (straight or gay) and conclude, "Nope, that's not right for us." After all, people read the Bible without deciding to acquire concubines. More realistically, they often encounter neighbors with different cultural mores while still preferring—and sometimes having good reason to prefer—their own.

Then there's the fairness issue: The question of whether same-sex couples should be allowed to marry should no more hinge on the behavior of a subset of gay men than the question of whether Hollywood actors should be allowed to marry should hinge on the behavior of a subset of Hollywood actors. In terms of raw numbers, there are probably many more heterosexual "swingers" than there are gay men in open relationships, yet we still allow heterosexual couples (including swingers!) to marry. On what grounds, then, can we deny marriage to same-sex couples, including those who pledge and achieve sexual exclusivity? The argument works even less well against gay sex than it does against same-sex marriage: The moral status of one person's sexual acts does not hinge on what other members of his or her sexual orientation do.

In short, the causal version of the PIB arguments fails, both as a prediction and as a moral objection.

Taboos and Moral Reasons

There is still another way of understanding the PIB argument. Maybe there's no direct logical connection between endorsing homosexuality and endorsing PIB. And maybe the gay-rights movement won't have much effect, one way or another, on the polygamy movement. Still, the very process of challenging existing sexual mores invites the following concern: If we start questioning *some* sexual taboos, won't that make it more likely that we'll start questioning others? Perhaps some things are best left unquestioned.[18]

If that's the objection, then much of this chapter has missed the point. We've been comparing reasons for and against homosexuality with reasons for and against PIB. But some might worry that once we start demanding *reasons* for established moral claims, morality has already lost its essential majesty and force. This objection is a version of the argument from tradition, but it's more sophisticated than the simple assertion, "We've always done it this way, therefore we should continue doing it this way." Rather, the idea is that our moral traditions have an internal practical logic to them, even when it's not apparent on the surface. They evolved the way they did for a *reason*, and tinkering with them invites peril.[19]

It is worth noting that just because something evolved as it did for a reason, it does not follow that it evolved as it did for a *good* reason. One of my favorite stories comes from the late food critic Craig Claiborne: A woman received a ham and was disappointed that she didn't own a saw.[20] Although she had never cooked a whole ham, she knew that her mother always prepared hams for cooking by sawing off the end, and she assumed it had to be done this way. So she called her mother, who explained that she learned to cook from her mother, who always did it that way—she had no idea why. The perplexed pair then called Grandma: "Why did you always saw the ends off of hams before roasting them?" they asked her.

---

18. I'm indebted to my colleague Brad Roth in the Wayne State Political Science department for pressing this reading of the PIB objection.

19. Rauch refers to this as a Hayekian argument. See Rauch, pp. 162–71.

20. Claiborne, p. 41.

Surprised, the old woman replied, "Because I never had a roasting pan large enough to hold a whole ham!"

The problem with the argument from tradition, even in its more sophisticated form, is that it takes a good point too far. All else being equal, there's a good reason to favor "tried and true" practices, and it would be impractical, even foolhardy, for each generation to invent morality from scratch. So I would agree that we should proceed with caution when tampering with long-standing tradition. But it doesn't follow that we can *never* revisit moral traditions. Take, for example, the taboo against interracial relationships, which has appeared in many cultures to varying degrees. We can understand how this taboo might have arisen, from an overzealous collective instinct for group preservation. There may, indeed, be a further "internal logic" behind it. Yet somehow we also recognize that the taboo causes needless pain and that it ought to be discarded.

My point here is not to suggest a perfect analogy (no analogy is perfect) but to invoke some lessons from history.[21] When a taboo interferes with people's happiness with no apparent justification, it is probably time to rethink it. Traditions have value, but so too does the process of ongoing moral reflection. We should not confuse reasonable caution with obstinate complacency, which can sometimes be a cover for bigotry (one of the topics in our next chapter).

The process is challenging, to be sure, and there are no shortcuts. It's easy to draw lines around things we don't like and then condemn others for falling outside the lines; it's much harder to articulate a coherent, complete, and plausible sexual ethics. It's especially hard to do so when people keep changing the subject—which, in the end, seems to be the PIB argument's main function.

---

21. See the conclusion of the previous chapter for some reflections on the race analogy.

7 | "BIGOTS, PERVERTS, AND THE REST OF US"

Glenn Stanton and I had just completed a debate at Hampden-Sydney College, probably the most conservative school I've ever visited. Founded in 1776, the all-male college regularly scores high on the Princeton Review's annual college poll in the category "Alternative Lifestyles Not an Alternative," meaning that it's not a friendly environment for gays. For my part, I received a relatively positive reception, although there were students in the audience who vocally objected to my presence. Glenn was gracious: After all, he's accustomed to being in the opposite position, where students object to *his* presence. College students tend to be more gay-friendly than their elders, and the overall national trend—especially among younger and educated populations—is in favor of letting same-sex couples marry.[1] In this chapter, I'll conclude the book by saying a bit more about the so-called culture wars, including the intersection between the marriage debate and the morality debate.

After the Hampden-Sydney event, I was driving Glenn back to our hotel when the conversation turned to our families. "My parents

---

1. "For First Time, Majority of Americans Favor Legal Gay Marriage," May 20, 2011, at http://www.gallup.com/poll/147662/first-timemajority-americans-favor-legal-gay-marriage.aspx.

are visiting Detroit next month," I mentioned. "They'll be in town for our commitment ceremony—oh, did I mention that? Mark and I are exchanging vows."

"Congratulations!" Glenn responded warmly.

I nearly swerved off the road.

I'm sure there are cynics who speculate that much of what Glenn and I do is pure theater: We get on stage, we recite our respective lines, and then we put it all aside when the audience isn't watching. But the cynics are wrong. What we say on stage, we deeply believe. And to the extent that we are able to maintain a friendship, it is only with effort and a heavy dose of tolerance. Each of us believes—and has argued, both publicly and privately—that the other promotes views that are harmful and wrong. Glenn, for example, has written that homosexuality is "a particularly evil lie of Satan"—and he stands by that claim. Which is why his "congratulations" genuinely shocked me.

After we arrived at the hotel we sat in the parking lot for quite some time and discussed it. Was he endorsing my relationship with Mark? No, of course not—at least not to the degree that the relationship is romantic.

After some back-and-forth, here's how he explained it: "When your friends find something that makes them happy, you're happy for them. Mark obviously makes you happy, and he's a very nice guy. I don't approve of the sexual relationship, but my gut reaction is to be happy for you because this is something that you want—I'm happy that you're happy."

Some might find his explanation mealy-mouthed, but I'm willing to give the guy some credit. I couldn't maintain any sort of friendship with Glenn if I didn't think that our relationship was giving him some cognitive dissonance—a tension between his anti-gay moral convictions and the evidence before his eyes. Calling someone a friend should mean something, and among the things it means is that you're willing to take that person's experience seriously, even when it conflicts with your own presuppositions. In saying "congratulations"—and standing by it afterward, despite the tension—Glenn was trying to do that.

I've had similar experiences with Maggie Gallagher, founder of the National Organization for Marriage, whom I also regularly debate. (Indeed, after seven years of plowing the same ground, Glenn and I have mostly retired our debate, whereas Maggie, with whom I've recently completed a book, is joining me more frequently.) On the way to our first public debate, Maggie and I unexpectedly encountered each other on a connecting flight in Salt Lake City, and we decided to sit together on the plane. At one point I pulled out my phone and showed her a picture of Mark, displaying his trademark broad smile.

"I can see why you call him home," she said.

At first I misunderstood her. "I don't need to call home," I answered. "I just talked to him."

"No—I can see why you call *him* home. He's 'home' for you," she replied.

Say what? As the National Organization for Marriage's co-founder, Maggie Gallagher has probably done more than any other single individual to ensure that, in the eyes of the law, Mark is *not* home for me. And yet, at some level, she too seems to "get it."

Moments like these give me hope—not so much for winning over Maggie and Glenn, but rather for winning over the many fence-sitters who want to support same-sex couples but haven't quite figured out how to do so. (And I'm not giving up on Maggie and Glenn yet, either.) It's a statistical fact that when heterosexual people know real live gay and lesbian people, they are less likely to condemn homosexuality and more likely to support legal marriage for same-sex couples. Evidence matters.

Let me contrast my longtime experience with Glenn with my experience of another evangelical leader, a pastor of a large church. We met at a behind-the-scenes meeting of about two-dozen people involved in the same-sex marriage debate, from different sides. The organizers brought us together to discuss strategies for a more civil and productive public dialogue—a "common ground" effort. I personally thought the effort was largely a failure, mainly because too many people refused to step away from their canned talking points. For me, the most illuminating part occurred outside the conference, when four of us—from opposing sides—stayed up late one night and engaged in some real conversation while polishing off a bottle of Scotch. In whisky, veritas.

Anyway, at one point in the conference the pastor gave a little speech about how he was grateful for the friendships he had just formed and how he was pleased to look around the room and to call all these people his friends . . . and all I could think was, "This guy is full of it." (It's too bad I hadn't yet started drinking, because I might have said so out loud.) His bit about friendship was just another canned talking point, and he seemed about as sincere as a stereotypical used-car salesman. He was throwing around the word "friend" as if friendship were cheap and easy. It isn't. True friendship takes effort. It requires vulnerability and a willingness to listen. I had no evidence that he was willing to make that kind of effort, and indeed, everything I had observed about him, both in the conference and in his public work, suggested otherwise. I may be on "friendly terms" with this pastor, but he is not my friend, and I am not his.

There are different kinds and degrees of friendship. There are professional friendships and personal friendships, deep friendships and casual friendships. Glenn and I, like Maggie and I, are more than just "acquaintances"—we've spent far too much time together and have had too many deep conversations for that—but we're not "best buds" either. Our friendship is a work in progress, fraught with tension and (at least on my part) doubt.

I recognize, too, that most readers know these people in a rather different way than I do, and our different vantage points may color our reactions. In many observers' minds, Glenn Stanton and Maggie Gallagher are inextricably linked to the powerful right-wing organizations which they represent: They're the "Focus-on-the-Family guy" and the "NOM lady." Yes, but they are also complex human individuals.

Some might wonder how I could be any sort of a friend with someone who vocally opposes same-sex relationships. It's complicated, and just as I reject cheap notions of friendship, I also reject easy answers to this question.

The following anecdote might help clarify some of the struggle involved. Glenn and I were once interviewed for a segment on the Christian Broadcasting Network's 700 Club program: "Friendliness Key to the Gay Marriage Debate?"[2] Although the reporter's efforts were well intentioned, I was troubled by the final product. It made the issue appear too neat and tidy—a "why can't we all just get along?" theme. Then there was the framing: the host, Gordon Robertson (son of the better-known Pat), seemed to want to contrast this nice, well-behaved gay man (me) with all those angry homosexual protestors rallying against California's Prop. 8, which stripped marriage rights from same-sex couples. In my view, LGBT Californians and their allies had good reason to be upset, and they channeled their anger in mostly productive ways.

My least favorite part of the segment occurred when Glenn noted how surprised audiences are that we call each other friends,

---

2. "Friendliness Key to the Gay Marriage Debate?" http://www.cbn.com/CBNnews/558119.aspx.

and he added sardonically, "Since when did we develop the rule that you can't hang out with people that you disagree with? That's amazing." I began to interject, but the camera cut away. My missing interjection explained why things aren't quite so simple: The issues we disagree on are deeply personal, and friendship is one way in which we express our values: If I have serious moral objections to someone's choices, I may properly express my disapproval by withholding friendship. It's not just about "hanging out" with a person, which can happen for all kinds of reasons, but about giving a certain blessing: this person is special to me.

At the same time, friendship is also about "clicking" with someone, which is not a rational process. If there's one thing that gay people ought to understand, it's that personal affection doesn't always line up with social expectations. Sometimes, against all odds, you simply find someone likable—even if you also find him exasperating. In this respect, friendships can be similar to family relationships, which often involve balancing self-protection alongside openness to others.

Who's Demonizing Whom?

One thing Gordon Robertson lamented in the 700 Club segment was the increasing tendency to "demonize" those with whom we disagree. It was an interesting choice of words. He was referring mainly to Prop. 8 protesters, but one might argue that Glenn has more literally demonized gay people by referring to homosexuality as a "particularly evil lie of Satan."

His claim appears on the Focus on the Family website, in an essay titled, "How We Dishonor God in Our Sex Lives." Homosexuality is not the central focus: On the same page Glenn calls premarital and extramarital sex a "monstrosity" and similarly rejects masturbation, pornography, and (not surprisingly) rape. Nevertheless, he seems to want to single out homosexuality for special condemnation:

> All sexual sin is wrong because it fails to mirror the Trinitarian image, but homosexuality does more than fail. It's a particularly evil lie of Satan because he knows that it overthrows the very image of the Trinitarian God in creation, revealed in the union of male and female.

> This is why this issue has become such a flashpoint. It will become even more contentious because nothing else challenges this image of the Triune God so profoundly and thoroughly as homosexuality. It's not what we were made for.[3]

In logic class we teach that anything can follow from a contradiction, so it probably shouldn't surprise me as a philosopher that people read whatever conclusions they want into the doctrine of the Trinity: "God is three persons . . . but God is one person." It's the ultimate theological mystery, and even its staunchest adherents admit that, at least on the surface, it makes no logical sense. But what does it have to do with sex? The idea seems that because God is *relational*, we mirror God most fully in our relationships. In that case, however, Glenn's discussion fails on its own terms: masturbation, which is not relational, would seem to "challenge the image of the Triune God" more "profoundly and thoroughly" than homosexuality.

---

3. Stanton, Glenn. "How We Dishonor God in Our Sex Lives," focusonthefamily.com June 27, 2012 at http://www.focusonthefamily.com/marriage/sex_and_intimacy/gods_ design_for_sex/how_we_dishonor_god_in_our_sex_lives.aspx.

In any case, I'm not interested in debating a theological point. (Like I said, people tend to read whatever they want into the doctrine of the Trinity. I'm still waiting for some radical lefty theologian to use it as an argument for three-way polyamory.) For the moment, I'm interested in the rhetoric.

Glenn, like other orthodox Christians, believes that all sin is from Satan. But he writes that homosexuality is a *particularly evil* lie of Satan because *nothing else* challenges this image of the Triune God so profoundly and thoroughly. For him to claim later that he's not picking uniquely on homosexuality rings false in light of his chosen words.

This debate doesn't happen in a vacuum. When someone calls homosexuality a particularly evil lie of Satan—right on the internet, on the Focus on the Family website—the statement has a profoundly harmful impact on gay and lesbian teens. Sloppy theology aside, and good intentions notwithstanding, here's what these kids will hear: Your deep longings for intimacy are not merely immoral or unwholesome, but *demonic*. Many of these kids pray desperately (but unsuccessfully) to be free from same-sex attraction. True, their heterosexual peers have similarly been told that Satan is behind their stubborn desires to masturbate or fornicate or view pornography. But from a gay teen's perspective, those heterosexual desires look like "normal" temptations, the ones that Satan visits on "normal" people like their schoolmates and pastors: The "particularly evil" desires must be reserved for particularly evil people.

I speak from personal experience. There was no internet when I was a teenager, so instead, I wandered into libraries and hid among the stacks, perusing whatever books I could find about sexual ethics. (I would never dare check one out.) Most of them reinforced the notion that there was something deeply wrong with me—not just in the general sense of "all humans have sinned and fallen short of the glory of God," but in the specific sense that gay feelings were a moral stain of the highest magnitude—a *perversion*, something that literally makes God sick. I cannot emphasize enough how emotionally scarring such rhetoric is. Moreover, the very people to whom teenagers might normally turn for solace—their parents, teachers, and ministers—often use this rhetoric most freely and unthinkingly. Gay teens are thus isolated from their natural support network, which compounds their cumulative sense of stigma.

When Gordon Robertson complains about gay-rights advocates "demonizing" their opponents, I want to hold up a mirror—to Robertson, to his father, to Stanton, to Dr. James Dobson (Focus's founder), and to every other member of the religious right who singles out homosexuality as particularly evil. If you're not willing to tone down the rhetoric, at least own up to what you're saying, and stop complaining about being demonized. There are limits to the common ground we can find here: I want to tell young LGBT people: *There is nothing wrong with you.* But the religious right cannot do that, at least not without reexamining some fundamental beliefs.

And yes, I've explained all this to Glenn Stanton. I've said repeatedly that if Focus on the Family and Christian conservatives would spend as much time emphasizing the "love thy neighbor" and "equal dignity" messages for gay people as they do the "homosexuality is evil" message, the world would be a much better place. (It would also make for a far more compelling Christian witness, though it's hardly my place to give them PR advice.) Jim Daly's replacement of Dobson as Focus's president has contributed to a positive change in tone, but the "particularly evil lie of Satan" line is still on their website, and it remains one of the most difficult points in our ongoing relationship.

Are They Bigots?

When people are unwilling to approve of same-sex relationships, does that make them *bigots*?

I believe in using the word "bigot" judiciously. Like "evil lie of Satan," it's a conversation-stopper, and we need more conversation around these issues, not less. To call someone a bigot is not merely to describe him or her as irrationally bound to false views; it's to label those views as beyond the pale. One does not thoughtfully entertain bigoted views any more than one thoughtfully entertains Satan's lies: one rejects them and keeps moving.

Gays did not invent the use of conversation-stopping rhetoric. Whenever someone labels us *perverts*, *deviants*, *agents of Satan*, or worse, they are casting us outside the realm of civilized discourse, and (wittingly or unwittingly) giving cover to those who would treat us as less than human. I know whereof I speak. I've had food thrown at me by people yelling "faggot." I've been physically attacked by teenage gay-bashers. And—twisted as it may sound— I've heard people invoke the Bible while doing such things.

Meaning well is not the same as *doing well*, as any honest look at history will reveal. I am reminded of my beloved grandparents, who— like many other whites of their generation—opposed interracial relationships. I admired and respected my grandparents. (Still do— one is still living.) Their racism was not the sneering, epithet-wielding, block-the-schoolhouse-door variety. Their stated reasons against inter-racial relationships sounded principled and wholesome: It's bad for the children, they'd say, or it's not what God wants, or sometimes: "It's just not right." They didn't make a fuss about it, and they didn't organize around it politically, but as a moral matter, they deeply believed it.

Were my grandparents bigots? I can certainly understand why many would think so. As someone who loves and was loved by them, I prefer to frame it this way: My grandparents—*like all of us, me included*—had their moral blind spots, and racism was among them.

My awareness of our shared human frailty is one reason you'll never hear me refer to gay rights as "the last frontier in the civil rights debate," as some do. Calling it the "last" implies that we, unlike our ancestors, have identified all our moral blind spots. But the whole point of calling them "blind spots" is that *we don't see them.* Just as belief in an infallible God doesn't make anyone infallible, belief in the moral demands of justice doesn't make anyone perfectly just.

Bigotry results from complacency at least as often as from malice. It can have a gracious, even noble-looking face. It's not necessarily about yelling epithets, or throwing food at people, or physically blocking doors. Sometimes it involves kindly grandparents who can't quite wrap their minds around social change. Sometimes it's about blocking metaphorical doors, rather than physical ones—which brings me to my final topic.

Conclusion: Love and Marriage

In the last two decades, the gay-rights debate has evolved into a debate over marriage. This is a natural evolution. In 1992, when I started speaking about gay rights, it was against the law in approximately two-dozen states for me to have private consensual relations with a same-sex partner: Indeed, for many years, I lived as an un-apprehended felon in the state of Texas. The option of *marrying* a same-sex partner was scarcely on anyone's radar. And so gay-rights rhetoric largely focused on freedom and privacy, a "leave us alone" message.

Telling anti-gay legislators to "leave us alone" made sense when we faced the threat of being harassed, jailed, and even put on sex-offender lists for private consensual lovemaking. But after the U.S. Supreme Court struck down sodomy laws in *Lawrence v. Texas* (2003), the "leave us alone" message became less relevant. It is not *irrelevant*—gays are still subjected to physical and emotional abuse, a tragedy that has become more apparent with the increased visibility of gay teen suicides—but it is less important as a political goal. Because marriage is a social institution, same-sex couples' desire to participate has changed our central public message from "leave us alone" to "include us." For better or for worse, this new message broaches the morality debate: As I explained above, people express their moral values in the associations they choose to keep, or not to keep.

The connection between the morality debate and the marriage debate is not absolute. One can believe that homosexuality is morally wrong while also believing that same-sex couples should have the legal freedom to marry, just as one can believe that divorce is morally wrong while also believing that a free society should permit it. Conversely, one can oppose same-sex marriage without believing that homosexuality is morally wrong (although the position is rare). But part of what marriage does as a social institution is to give a kind of public moral blessing to otherwise private commitments, and so the two debates are inextricably entwined.

This moral dimension of marriage is one reason the issue is so contentious. When same-sex couples ask for marriage, they are not only asking for legal rights and responsibilities—although those are crucial, and their denial can be devastating—they are also asking for inclusion, affirmation, and equal respect. No one should be ashamed to seek such things: Human beings are social creatures. But it's important to remember that, given the affirmative message that marriage carries, asking for it means asking others to confer something. It's not just a personal relationship between spouses; it's also a relationship between the couple and the community. For gays, it's about access to an institution that our heterosexual fellow citizens take largely for granted.

Of course, the state cannot legitimately force anyone to condone anyone else's relationship decisions. In a free society, citizens retain the right to opine as they wish on homosexuality, marriage, or any other topic. Yet citizens of a free society also expect equal treatment under the law, and they must accept that others may exercise freedom in ways they themselves don't necessarily approve. For example, you might believe that interfaith marriage is immoral, or that divorce and remarriage are immoral. You might believe that your daughter's fiancé is a jerk and that for her to marry him would be just plain wrong. You might think that there should be a moratorium on Kardashian weddings. You are entitled to your convictions, but in the United States, at least, you may not stop anyone from marrying because of them.

I'm not going to rehearse the arguments for and against same-sex marriage here. (I've recently done so at length with Maggie Gallagher in our book together.) I simply want to emphasize that, at its core, the marriage debate is a moral debate: It's about the kind of relationships society is willing to embrace—or, short of that, to tolerate. It is about the fact that relationships are good for people, that social support is good for relationships, and that some people find love with persons of the same sex. Although it involves legal rights and responsibilities, it's about more than that: It is one thing for the state to let you marry, and quite another for your family to show up at your wedding and be happy for you. In my view, both elements are important.

In these pages I've argued that there is no good reason to condemn same-sex relationships, and that, indeed, there's a good reason to affirm them: Like their heterosexual counterparts, they can be an important avenue of human well-being. As someone who has been involved in this debate for two decades, I recognize that philosophical argument only takes us so far, and that this issue demands not merely a change of mind but also a change of heart. But nor should we dismiss the value of reasoned discourse in opening a space for a broader personal and social transformation. When moral arguments are twisted into weapons, as happens all too often, philosophical analysis becomes more than merely relevant: It becomes morally urgent. I hope that this book invites an ongoing dialogue that is thoughtful, rigorous, sensitive, and productive.

ACKNOWLEDGMENTS

This book is the product of two decades of speaking, writing, and debating about same-sex relationships. It grew out of a lecture, "What's Morally Wrong with Homosexuality?," which I first presented as a graduate student at the University of Texas at Austin in 1992 and have since delivered, in various incarnations, at well over 100 universities across the country. (The lecture is available on DVD; you can watch the trailer at www.johncorvino.com.)

Given this long history, it is impossible for me to recall, let alone properly thank, the countless audience members, colleagues, friends and critics who have contributed to this book's development. Let me here mention those who provided helpful comments on recent drafts, in part or in full: Matthew Lee Anderson, David Baggett, Ron Belgau, Jim Burroway, Paul Clemens, Maggie Gallagher, Sherif Girgis, Christie Herring, Kevin Lamb, Karen Mottola, Timothy Hulsey, Jessica Pettitt, Jonathan Rauch, and Glenn Stanton.

My colleagues in the Wayne State University philosophy department (and other departments) have provided me with a lively work environment of enviable rigor—I am grateful to them for helping me to sharpen many of this book's arguments. I am also grateful for the generous support and exceptional integrity of the staff at Oxford University Press, especially Peter Ohlin, Lucy Randall, Justyna Zajac, Allison Finkel, and Lisa Force, along with various anonymous reviewers.

If there's one point on which the "religious right" and I firmly agree, it's the importance of family. Mine has been exceptional. Mom, Dad, Jen, Grandpa Joe: I could not have done my work of the last twenty years without your support, as well as that of Grandma Rose, Grandpa John, and Grandma Tess, who are very much missed. I am also grateful for a large and loving extended family, including a close group of Detroit friends who have become family.

When I first came out of the closet as a gay man nearly 25 years ago, in addition to the invaluable support of family and friends, I was blessed with a role model whose mentoring was pivotal: a Franciscan priest named Fr. Richard Cardarelli. Fr. Richard died just as I was preparing the final draft of this book. I hope that in some way it pays forward my profound debt to him.

Last, but certainly not least, there's my partner, Mark, who sustains me each day with unwavering patience, confidence, and care. I dedicate this book to him, with love.

BIBLIOGRAPHY

APA Task Force on Appropriate Therapeutic Responses to Sexual Orientation. *Report of the Task Force on Appropriate Therapeutic Responses to Sexual Orientation*. Washington, DC: American Psychological Association, 2009. Accessed June 27, 2012 at http://www.apa.org/pi/lgbt/resources/therapeutic-response.pdf.

Aquinas, St. Thomas. *Summa Contra Gentiles*. Book 3 (Providence). Part II translated by Vernon J. Bourke. Notre Dame, IN: University of Notre Dame Press, 1975.

———. *Summa Theologica*. Westminster, MD: Christian Classics, 1981.

Bagemihl, Bruce. *Biological Exuberance: Animal Homosexuality and Natural Diversity*. New York: St. Martin's Press, 1999.

Bailey, Nathan W., and Marlene Zuk. "Same-Sex Sexual Behavior and Evolution." *Trends in Ecology & Evolution* 24, no. 8 (Aug. 2009): 439–46.

Beachy, S. "20+, HIV+." *New York Times Magazine*, April 17, 1994, 52–53.

Bentham, Jeremy. "An Essay on 'Paederasty,'" in Robert Baker and Frederick Elliston, eds., *The Philosophy of Sex*. Buffalo, NY: Prometheus 1984.

Bhaskaran, Krishnan et. al. "Changes in the Risk of Death After HIV Seroconversion Compared With Mortality in the General Population." *Journal of the American Medical Association* 300, no. 1 (2008): 51–59.

Bowers v. Hardwick 478 U.S. 186 (1986).

Cameron, Paul, W.L. Playfair, and S. Wellum. "The Longevity of Homosexuals: Before and After the AIDS Epidemic." *Omega* 29 (1994): 249–72.

Carey, Benedict. "Psychiatry Giant Sorry for Backing Gay 'Cure.'" *New York Times*, May 18, 2012. Accessed June 27, 2012 at http://www.nytimes.com/2012/05/19/health/dr-robert-l-spitzer-noted-psychiatrist-apologizes-for-study-on-gay-cure.html?pagewanted=all.

Chappell, T. D. J. *Understanding Human Goods*. Edinburgh: Edinburgh University Press, 1995.

Claiborne, Craig. *The New New York Times Cookbook*. New York: Random House, 1995.

Coontz, Stephanie. Marriage: A History. New York: Viking, 2005.

Corvino, John. "By Their Fruits Ye Shall Know Them: Homosexuality, Biblical Revisionism, and the Relevance of Experience." In Mary Garrett, Heidi Gottfried, and Sandra F. VanBurkleo, eds., *Remapping the Humanities; Identity, Memory, Community, and (post)Modernity*. Detroit: Wayne State University Press, 2008, 59–72.

———. "Homosexuality and the PIB Argument." *Ethics* 115 (April 2005): 501–34.

———. "Homosexuality, Harm, and Moral Principles." In Laurence Thomas, ed., *Contemporary Debates in Social Philosophy*. Malden: Blackwell, 2007, 79–93.

———. "Richardson was Right—Sort of." igfculturewatch.com, August 8, 2007. Accessed June 23, 2012 at http://igfculturewatch.com/2007/08/20/richardson-was-right-sort-of/.

———. "Why Shouldn't Tommy and Jim Have Sex: A Defense of Homosexuality." In John Corvino, ed., *Same Sex: Debating the Ethics, Science, and Culture of Homosexuality*. Lanham, Md: Rowman & Littlefield, 1997.

——— and Maggie Gallagher. *Debating Same-Sex Marriage*. New York: Oxford University Press, 2012.

Crompton, Louis. *Homosexuality and Civilization*. Cambridge, MA: Harvard University Press, 2003.

"Excerpts of Santorum's AP Interview." Taped April 7, 2003, published April 22, 2003, by the Associated Press. http://www.foxnews.com/story/0,2933,84862,00.html.

Finnis, John. "Is Natural Law Theory Compatible with Limited Government?" in Robert P. George, ed., *Natural Law, Liberalism, and Morality*. Oxford: Oxford University Press, 1996.

———. "Law, Morality, and 'Sexual Orientation.'" In John Corvino, ed., *Same Sex: Debating the Ethics, Science, and Culture of Homosexuality*. Rowman & Littlefield: Lanham, MD: 1997, 31–43.

———. *Natural Law and Natural Rights*. Oxford: Oxford University Press, 1980.

"For First Time, Majority of Americans Favor Legal Gay Marriage." Gallup.com, May 20, 2011. http://www.gallup.com/poll/147662/first-time-majority-americans-favor-legal-gay-marriage.aspx.

"Friendliness Key to the Gay Marriage Debate?" CBN.com, June 1, 2009. Accessed June 27, 2012 at http://www.cbn.com/CBNnews/558119.aspx.

Frutkin, Alan. "The Gospel Truth?" *The Advocate* 747 (Nov. 25, 2007): 22.

Gagnon, Robert A. J., and Dan O Via. *Homosexuality and the Bible: Two Views*. Minneapolis: Fortress Press, 2003.

Gates, Gary J. "Gay People Count, So Why Not Count Them Correctly?" *Washington Post*, April 8, 2011. http://www.washingtonpost.com/opinions/gay-people-count-so-why-not-count-them-correctly/2011/04/07/AFDg9K4C_story.html.

George, Robert P. *In Defense of Natural Law*. Oxford: Oxford University Press, 1999.

———. "What's Sex Got to Do with It? Marriage, Morality, and Rationality" in Robert P. George and Jean Bethke Elshtain, eds., *The Meaning of Marriage: Family, State, Market and Morals*. Dallas: Spence, 2006.

Girgis, Sherif, Robert P. George, and Ryan T. Anderson. "What Is Marriage?" *Harvard Journal of Law and Public Policy* 34 (2010): 245.

Gomez-Lobo, Alfonso. *Morality and the Human Goods: An Introduction to Natural Law Ethics*, Washington, DC: Georgetown University Press, 2002.

Grisez, Germain. *The Way of the Lord Jesus, Volume I: Christian Moral Principles*. Chicago: Franciscan Herald Press, 1983.

———. *The Way of the Lord Jesus, Volume 2: Living a Christian Life*. Quincy, IL: Franciscan Press, 1993.

Halperin, David. *One Hundred Years of Homosexuality*. New York: Routledge, 1990.

Hogg, R. S. Letter to the *International Journal of Epidemiology* 30 (2001):1499.

Hogg, R. S., S. A. Strathdee, K. J. Craib, M. V. O'Shaughnessy, J. S. Montaner, and M. T. Schechter. "Modelling the Impact of HIV Disease on Mortality in Gay and Bisexual Men." *International Journal of Epidemiology* 26, no. 3 (Jun. 1997): 657–61.

Jordan, Mark D. *The Invention of Sodomy in Christian Theology*. Chicago: University of Chicago Press, 1997.

Koppelman, Andrew. *The Gay-Rights Question in Contemporary American Law*. Chicago: University of Chicago Press, 2002.

———. "Is Marriage Inherently Heterosexual?" *Am. J. of Jurisprudence* 42 (1997): 51.

Kurtz, Stanley. "Beyond Gay Marriage: The Road to Polyamory." *Weekly Standard*, August 4, 2003. Accessed September 7, 2012, at http://pages. pomona.edu/~vis04747/h21/readings/Kurz_Beyond_gay_marriage.pdf.

———. "Big Love: From the Set." *National Review*, March 13, 2006. Accessed September 7, 2012 at http://www.nationalreview.com/articles/217027/ i-big-love-i-set/stanley-kurtzhttp://old.nationalreview.com/kurtz/kurtz. asp.

Laumann, Edward O., John H. Gagnon, Robert T. Michael, and Stuart Michaels. *The Social Organization of Sexuality: Sexual Practices in the United States*. Chicago: University of Chicago Press, 2000.

Lawrence v. Texas, 539 U.S. 558 (2003).

Levin, Michael. "Homosexuality, Abnormality, and Civil Rights." *Public Affairs Quarterly* 10 no. 1 (Jan. 1996): 31–48.

———. "Why Homosexuality is Abnormal." *Monist* 67 (1984): 251–83.

Loving v. Virginia 388 U.S. 1 (1967).

Mohr, Richard D. *Gays/Justice: A Study of Ethics, Society, and the Law*. New York: Columbia University Press, 1988.

Murphy, Mark C. *Natural Law and Practical Rationality*. New York: Cambridge University Press, 2001.

Nissinen, Martti. *Homoeroticism in the Biblical World: A Historical Perspective*. Minneapolis: Fortress Press, 1998.

"Only the Gay Die Young? Part 2—Danish Epidemiologist Reviews the Cameron Study." wthrockmorton.com, April 13, 2007. Accessed June 27, 2012 at http://wthrockmorton.com/2007/04/13/only-the-gay-die-young-part-2-danish-epidemiologist-reviews-the-cameron-study/.

The Ramsey Colloquium. "The Homosexual Movement." *First Things* (March 1994):15–20.

Rauch, Jonathan. *Gay Marriage: Why It Is Good for Gays, Good for Straights, and Good For America*. New York: Times Books, 2004.

Ryan, Caitlan, David Huebner, Rafael M. Diaz, and Jorge Sanchez, "Family Rejection as a Predictor of Negative Health Outcomes in White and Latino Lesbian, Gay, and Bisexual Young Adults, Pediatrics Vol. 123 No. 1 January 1, 2009 pp. 346–352.

Stanton, Glenn. "How We Dishonor God in Our Sex Lives." focusonthefamily. com. Accessed June 27, 2012 at http://www.focusonthefamily.com/marriage/sex_and_intimacy/gods_design_for_sex/how_we_dishonor_god_in_our_sex_lives.aspx.

Stein, Edward. *The Mismeasure of Desire: The Science, Theory, and Ethics of Sexual Orientation*. New York: Oxford University Press, 2001.

Sullivan, Andrew, ed. *Same-Sex Marriage: Pro and Con: A Reader*. New York: Vintage Books, 1997.

"Texas Officer Suspended for Comment to Gay Couple." Associated Press, December 10, 2004. http://austin.ynn.com/content/top_stories/126767/capitol-trooper-disciplined-for-comment-to-gay-couple.

"'Therapies to Change Sexual Orientation Lack Medical Justification And Threaten Health." Pan American Health Organization, May 17, 2012. Accessed June 27, 2012 at http://new.paho.org/hq/index.php?option=com_content&task=view&id=6803&Itemid=1926.

Thomas, Laurence M., and Michael E. Levin. *Sexual Orientation and Human Rights*. Lanham, MD: Rowman & Littlefield, 1999.

Wolfe, Christopher. "Homosexual Acts, Morality, and Public Discourse." In Laurence Thomas, ed., *Contemporary Debates in Social Philosophy*. Malden: Blackwell, 2007, 94–110.

———. "Homosexuality in American Public Life," in Christopher Wolfe, ed. *Same-Sex Matters: The Challenge of Homosexuality*. Dallas: Spence, 2000.

INDEX

HIV/AIDS (human
        immunodeficiency virus
        infection/acquired
        immunodeficiency syndrome),
        50–52, 55–59, 66, 74, 75
homophobia
    avoidance of gay company, 72–76
    harm arguments against
        homophobia, 76
    racism *vs.* homophobia, 119
"Homosexuality and the PIB
        Argument," 128
"The Homosexual Life span," 52
humiliation and degradation, 30–32
humility, kindness, and love in Biblical
        teaching, 38, 45

Idaho, 2–5
incest
    in PIB (polygamy, incest, and
        bestiality) argument, 122–131
"infertile couples" objection, 90
infidelity and adultery, 38, 39, 46, 84,
        121, 122, 134, 135
interracial relationships, 97, 130, 137,
        147
intimacy, 17, 67, 86, 94, 95, 114, 125,
        126, 145
isolation, 58, 146
    academic isolationism, 11

*Journal of the American Medical
        Association,* 56
joy
    genuine human goods, 16, 126
    moral value in, 17

See also happiness; pleasure and
        gratification
Judges (biblical story), 30
judging one another
    morality as public concern, 6, 7
    resulting isolation, 58

Kant, Immanuel, 86, 87, 94
kindness
    Bible
        love, kindness, and humility in,
            38, 45
        humility, kindness, and love in
            Biblical teaching, 38, 45
kissing, 2, 13, 32, 59, 79, 96, 107
Koppelman, Andrew, 72, 95
Kurtz, Stanley, 132, 133

Lawrence v. Texas, 121, 123, 149
laws governing homosexual conduct,
        121
    civil/equal rights under law, 148, 150
    Proposition 8 (California), 142, 143
    sodomy laws, 148, 149
Laws (Plato), 78
Lee, Patrick, 87, 94
lesbian sex, 32–34
    HIV transmission, likelihood, 57
Levin, Michael, 59–61, 67–76
Leviticus, 30–36, 40, 44, 46
LGBT (lesbian, gay, bisexual,
        transgender) distinctions,
        14, 15
life expectancy of gays, 49, 52–56
"lifestyle" of homosexuality *vs.*
        homosexual sex, 13, 14